GRILL BY THE BOOK

Fish and Shellfish

By the Editors of Sunset Books

with special contributions by

Jerry Anne Di Vecchio
and
Betty Hughes

Sunset Books Inc.
Menlo Park, California

President & Publisher:
Susan J. Maruyama

Director, Sales & Marketing:
Richard A. Smeby

Director, New Business:
Kenneth Winchester

Editorial Director:
Bob Doyle

Marketing & Creative Services Manager:
Guy C. Joy

Production Director:
Lory Day

EDITORIAL STAFF FOR FISH AND SHELLFISH

Coordinating Editor:
Lynne Gilberg

Research & Text:
Paula Smith Freschet

Consulting Editor:
Betty Hughes, Director, Consumer Affairs, Weber-Stephen Products Co.

Contributing Editors:
Sandra Cameron
Barbara Sause
Cynthia Scheer

Copy Editor:
Fran Feldman

Editorial Assistant:
Jody Mitori

Photography:
Chris Shorten

Food Stylists:
Heidi Gintner
Susan Massey
Dianne Torrie
Sue White

Food Styling Assistant:
Andrea Lucich

Prop Stylist:
Laura Ferguson

Design:
Don Komai, Watermark Design

Page Layout:
Dayna Goforth

Recipe Testers:
Susan Block
Dorothy Decker
Barbara Gobar
Aileen Russell
Jean Strain
Linda Tebben

SUNSET PUBLISHING CORPORATION

Chairman:
Jim Nelson

President & Chief Executive Officer:
Stephen J. Seabolt

Chief Financial Officer:
James E. Mitchell

Publisher, Sunset Magazine:
Anthony P. Glaves

Director of Finance:
Larry Diamond

Circulation Director:
Robert I. Gursha

Vice President, Manufacturing:
Lorinda Reichert

Editor, Sunset Magazine:
William Marken

Senior Editor, Food & Entertaining:
Jerry Anne Di Vecchio

The kettle grill configuration is a registered trademark of WEBER-STEPHEN PRODUCTS CO.

The GENESIS®, PERFORMER®, SMOKEY JOE®, and GO ANYWHERE® grill configurations are trademarks of WEBER-STEPHEN PRODUCTS CO.

For more information on *Grill by the Book* or any other Sunset book, call 800-526-5111.

Fourth printing December 1997

A word about our nutritional data

For our recipes, we provide a nutritional analysis stating calorie count; percentage of calories from fat; grams of total fat and saturated fat; milligrams of cholesterol and sodium; grams of carbohydrates, fiber, and protein; and milligrams of calcium and iron. Generally, the analysis applies to a single serving, based on the number of servings given for each recipe and the amount of each ingredient. If a range is given for the number of servings and/or the amount of an ingredient, the analysis is based on the average of the figures given.

The nutritional analysis does not include optional ingredients or those for which no specific amount is stated. If an ingredient is listed with a substitution, the information was calculated using the first choice.

Contents

The Art of Grilling

page 4

Recipes

page 15

Index

page 64

Special Features

The Art of Grilling

Some folks say opposites attract, and I suppose that's how it was when Weber met Sunset. Weber is a Chicago-area company with a long tradition of forming steel into very durable barbecue grills. Sunset is a San Francisco-area company with a long tradition of forming words and photographs into informative and entertaining publications.

Weber's roots are in the Midwest, and I guess that means we really appreciate a good, thick steak and meaty ribs from the heartland. Sunset's roots are in California, where fresh Pacific seafood and an almost infinite variety of vegetables abound.

Now, even if opposites attract they must have something in common for a long-term relationship to develop.

You see, at Weber we believe you ought to buy one of our products and be pleasantly surprised that it exceeds your expectations. Sunset thinks the same way. When they write a recipe, the amount of testing they do to make sure it'll come out just so is mind-boggling.

About a year ago, Weber decided to produce a series of cookbooks to help backyard chefs have more fun with their grills. Sunset was considering a similar project. So, when we shared our mutual desire to write a series of simply great barbecue cookbooks, we decided we could make them even better if we formed a partnership.

We believe that this terrific cookbook will help you have fun with your grill, but if you have any suggestions for improvements, simply give us a call at the following number: (800) 446-1071. Your comments will help us get better at what we do, and we want to make sure you're totally satisfied with our products.

Mike Kempster

Michael Kempster, Sr.
Executive Vice President
Weber-Stephen Products Co.

A Range of Grill Options

Today's Weber® Grills come in a range of sizes, models, and prices, that offer backyard chefs a myriad of options. Before you purchase a grill, however, it's important to consider your cooking objectives. The grills described below offer a variety of convenient features that may be important to you.

No matter which Weber® model you choose, however, it's going to be a covered grill. The lid gives you the flexibility of using either the Direct or Indirect Methods of cooking. It also allows you to utilize more heat, reduces the amount of cooking time, and virtually eliminates flare-ups.

Weber® One-Touch® Charcoal Kettle

With the Weber® One-Touch® Kettle, one lever opens the vents to create the natural convection heat that helps seal in juices and flavor. The same lever also simplifies ash removal. Flip-up sides on the hinged cooking grate make it easy to add charcoal briquets while food cooks.

The kettle is available in two diameters: 18½ inches (47 cm) or 22½ inches (57 cm). Both offer plenty of cooking space.

Weber® Performer® Grill with Touch-N-Go™ Gas Ignition System

The ultimate ease in charcoal barbecuing begins with the exclusive gas ignition system on this grill, which makes quick work of lighting charcoal briquets. All you do is push a button. A high-capacity ash catcher makes cleaning easy, too. The large charcoal storage container keeps charcoal dry.

This model also has the Dual-Purpose Thermometer, the Tuck-Away™ Lid Holder, and Char-Basket™ Fuel Holders.

Weber®, Smokey Joe®, and Go-Anywhere® Grills

Smaller in size than the other Weber® grills, these transportable tabletop models cook the same way as their larger counterparts. They are available in charcoal and gas models.

Weber® Genesis® 3000 Series Gas Barbecue Grill

A convenient alternative to cooking with charcoal, this grill features specially angled Flavorizer® Bars that distribute the heat evenly and vaporize the drippings to create barbecue flavor without flare-ups. Stainless steel burners run the length of the cooking box, offering controlled, even cooking and energy efficiency.

This grill has 635 square inches (4,097 square cm) of cooking area and warming racks. Its durable porcelain-enameled cooking grate is easy to clean.

Other features include the Dual-Purpose Thermometer, weather-resistant wood work surfaces, and an easy-to-read fuel scale. Available in liquid propane and natural gas models.

Grilling Techniques

The Direct Method in a Charcoal Kettle

This grilling technique is best for relatively thin pieces of food that cook in less than 25 minutes; many fish fillets, fish steaks, and shellfish fall in this category. Direct cooking is also used for steaks, chops, burgers, boneless chicken breasts, and turkey tenderloins. The food is placed directly over hot coals.

To prepare the grill, open all of the vents and spread charcoal briquets in a single solid layer that fills the charcoal grate. Next, mound the briquets in a pyramid-shaped pile and ignite them, keeping the lid off. When the briquets are lightly coated with gray ash (25 to 30 minutes), use long-handled tongs to spread them into a single layer again. Set the cooking grate in place and arrange the food on the grate. Place the lid on the grill, leaving all vents open, and grill as directed in your recipe, turning the food once halfway through the cooking time.

The Direct Method in a Gas Barbecue

With gas grills, use of the Direct Method is limited to preheating and searing; the latter technique, while useful for certain cuts of meat and poultry, is not used for fish or shellfish. All of the actual grilling in this book will be done by the Indirect Method.

To preheat the grill, open the lid and check that all burner control knobs are turned to OFF and the fuel scale reads more than "E." Turn on the gas at the source. Light with the igniter switch or, if necessary, a match (see the manufacturer's directions). Check through the viewing port to be sure the burner is lit. Close the lid, turn all burners to HIGH, and preheat 10 to 15 minutes to bring the grill to 500°–550°F (260°–288°C). Then adjust the heat controls as the recipe directs and proceed to cook the food.

Tips for Cooking Seafood on a Grill

- *Firm-textured fish fillets and steaks can be placed directly on the cooking grate. Less sturdy types need the support of a piece of heavy-duty foil. Cut the foil just large enough to hold the fish without crowding.*

- *Some soft-textured whole fish and large fillets also need extra support. Place them, skin side down, on a piece of heavy-duty foil. Cut the foil to follow the outlines of the fish, leaving a 1- to 2-inch border. Crimp the foil to fit against the fish. Use a wide metal spatula with a long handle to turn fish on the grill and to transfer it to a platter or plates.*

- *For kebabs, choose nonflaky fish or fish with firm, dense flesh, such as halibut, lingcod, sea bass, shark, swordfish, and tuna. Otherwise, pieces will more than likely fall off the skewers. You can also skewer large scallops or shelled, deveined shrimp. Note: In a charcoal grill, use about three-quarters of the amount of briquets you would normally use—one layer of sparsely arranged coals will provide just the right heat for kebabs.*

- *If you're using bamboo skewers for kebabs, soak them in water for 30 minutes before skewering to prevent the wood from charring.*

Indirect Cooking in a Charcoal Kettle

Use this method for whole fish and thick-cut fish fillets that need to cook for more than 25 minutes at lower temperatures. The same technique will be used for roasts, ribs, and a variety of poultry preparations. The food is not turned, and the grill must be kept covered, since every time you open the lid, heat escapes and the cooking time increases.

To set up the grill for the Indirect Method, open all vents. Position Char-Basket™ Fuel Holders or charcoal rails on either side of the charcoal grate as close as possible to the outside edges. Divide the charcoal briquets evenly and place them in the holders (see the chart below for the number to use). Ignite the briquets and, keeping the lid off, let them burn until lightly covered with gray ash (25 to 30 minutes). If necessary, use long-handled tongs to rearrange briquets so the heat will be even.

Place a foil drip pan on the charcoal grate between the baskets of coals. Put the cooking grate in place, positioning the hinged sides of the grate over the briquets so that more can be added if necessary. Arrange the food in the center of the cooking grate. Place the lid on the grill, leaving all vents open, and grill as directed. If the food is to cook for more than an hour, add briquets as indicated on the chart.

Indirect Cooking in a Gas Barbecue

The Indirect Method is always the best approach to cooking fish and shellfish on a gas grill. Turn the food only if you are directed to do so in the recipe. The grill must be kept covered or you will have to increase the cooking time. Let foods grill for the minimum time specified in the recipe before checking for doneness.

When using the Indirect Method, preheat as directed for the Direct Method (facing page). Arrange the food in the center of the cooking grate and place the lid on the grill. For three-burner grills, set the front and back burners to MEDIUM and the center burner to OFF; for two-burner grills, turn the front and back burners to MEDIUM.

If you have another brand of grill, check your owner's manual for Indirect cooking instructions.

Quick Smoke Flavoring

When you use a covered barbecue grill, wood chips or chunks placed beneath the cooking grate can add a delicate smoked flavor. Chips are ideal for foods with shorter cooking times; chunks are best for foods that take longer. The best woods for fish and shellfish are grapevine, hickory, oak, and mesquite. You may also want to experiment with orange peels, dried corn cobs, dried fennel stocks, garlic, or woody perennial fresh herbs.

Start by soaking the wood chips or chunks in water—30 minutes for chips, one hour for chunks.

In a charcoal grill, scatter a handful or two of the wet chips right over the hot coals. With a gas grill, turn the heat to HIGH and place the chips with a little bit of water in a small foil pan directly on the heat source in the left front corner of the grill. Used as directed, a Weber® Steam-N-Chips™ Smoker makes such quick smoking a snap. Preheat the barbecue as directed and cook by the Indirect Method on MEDIUM heat.

When the wood starts smoking, begin grilling, and keep the lid on. Add more soaked chips when you no longer see smoke exiting the vents. Remember, a little smoke goes a long way—you want the flavor to complement, not overpower, the food's natural taste.

The Right Amount of Charcoal for Indirect Cooking

Diameter of grill in inches	Briquets needed on each side for first hour	Number of briquets to add to each side every hour
26¾" (68 cm)	30	9
22½" (57 cm)	25	8
18½" (47 cm)	16	5

Fuels & Fire Starters

Charcoal briquets. Long the outdoor chef's favorite fuel, charcoal briquets are manufactured from pulverized charcoal and additives that make them easy to light. Once ignited, briquets provide good even heat, but the various brands differ somewhat in composition and density. Top-quality brands burn longer and more evenly. Store briquets in a dry place.

Self-starting briquets. Impregnated with a liquid starter, these briquets ignite with a match and heat up quickly. *Do not add self-starting briquets to an existing hot fire*—the fuel in them burns off slowly and it can spoil the flavor of the food. Always use regular briquets when additional charcoal is needed.

Liquid starter. If you use a liquid starter, be sure it's a product intended for charcoal, and follow the manufacturer's instructions closely. Let the starter soak into the coals for a few minutes; then ignite in several places. *Never* pour liquid starter on hot coals—this can cause a dangerous flare-up.

Solid starter. Solid starters such as Weber® FireStarters are safe, nontoxic, odorless cubes that light easily with a match and burn without further attention. Mound the briquets in a pyramid shape on top of the cubes, leaving a corner of the cubes exposed. Ignite the cubes, and the coals will be ready in 25 to 30 minutes.

Chimney starter. The metal cannister on this device holds a supply of charcoal briquets a few inches above the charcoal grate. Light two Weber® FireStarters or some wadded newspapers underneath the chimney, and it will bring the coals quickly to readiness.

Electric starter. Comprised of a large heating element, a handle, and an electrical cord, this device nestles in a bed of unlit briquets and ignites them when the cord is connected. After 10 minutes, remove the starter (if you leave it in too long, the heating element will burn out).

Liquid propane and natural gas. Gas barbecues use either liquid propane or natural gas as fuel. Liquid propane is stored in a refillable tank mounted on the barbecue grill. Expect 20 to 30 hours of use from a tank. Natural gas is piped to a grill through a permanent hookup to a gas line. *Note:* Never use one kind of fuel in a barbecue grill designed for the other.

Fire Safety

Follow the manufacturer's instructions carefully and heed the rules below to ensure safety while you grill.

■ *Never leave a hot grill unattended. Keep children and pets at a safe distance.*

■ *Never use a charcoal or gas grill indoors or in a closed garage or enclosed patio.*

■ *Do not use gasoline or other highly volatile fluids as charcoal lighters. Do not add liquid starter to hot—or even warm—coals.*

■ *Place your grill in an open, level area away from the house, wood railings, trees, bushes, or other combustible surfaces. Do not attempt to barbecue in high winds.*

■ *Wear an insulated, fire-retardant barbecue mitt and use long-handled tools designed for grilling. Do not wear clothing with loose, flowing sleeves.*

Buying & Storing Fish & Shellfish

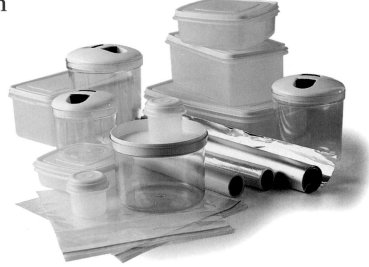

Freshness is the key to quality in fish and shellfish. From the moment it leaves the water to the time it reaches your market, seafood must be handled properly; if it hasn't been treated well, you'll know by aroma and appearance.

Fresh and Frozen Seafood

Your nose is the most reliable judge of freshness; any disagreeable, sweet, or ammonialike odors are caused by bacteria that proliferate as seafood deteriorates.

Fresh fish fillets and steaks should look moist, lustrous, and cleanly cut, as if they were just placed on display. The eyes of a fresh whole fish are clear, full, and often protruding; cloudy, sunken eyes indicate an old fish that's starting to spoil. The gills should be clean and red, not sticky and gray; scales should be shiny and tightly attached to the skin. The flesh should always feel firm and elastic.

It's more difficult to gauge the freshness of packaged fish, but if you can detect a strong odor through the packaging, don't buy it. Also avoid packages in which liquid has collected, especially if it's cloudy or off-white. If you're purchasing frozen fish, check that the flesh is solidly frozen with no discoloration, no buildup of ice crystals, and no evidence of drying. Packaging should be airtight and undamaged.

You know shellfish is fresh if it's alive and vigorous. If shellfish die naturally, they won't necessarily make you sick, but their meat spoils rapidly, so it's best to discard them. Enzymes in dead crabs work quickly in making them unfit to eat.

Fresh hard-shell clams, oysters, and mussels should have tightly closed shells—the best indication that they are still alive. If a shell is slightly open, it should close when gently tapped. Live crabs and lobsters should move their legs. Cooked crab or lobster should have a bright red shell and be free of any ammonialike aroma. Fresh scallops have a slightly sweet smell; their color varies from creamy white to tan or orange. If you buy packaged scallops, choose packages with little or no accumulated liquid. Fresh shrimp are firm in texture, with a mild, faintly sweet aroma; don't buy them if they smell of ammonia. Indications of mishandled shrimp include black legs, slippery shells, and shells with dark spots or dry-looking patches.

Make sure frozen shrimp, crab, or lobster tail is well glazed and not dried out; the meat should be white with no signs of yellowing.

How Much to Buy

From a strictly nutritional standpoint, the recommended serving of cooked, boneless seafood is about 3 ounces (85 g). Many people will enjoy eating more than that, however. For each person, figure on 5 to 8 ounces (140 to 230 g) of uncooked fish fillets or steaks; 8 ounces to 1 pound (230 to 455 g) of whole, cleaned fish; 1 to 1½ pounds (455 to 680 g) of mussels or clams in the shell; about 4 ounces (115 g) of shelled shrimp; 1 to 2 pounds (455 to 905 g) of whole live crab or lobster; or about 4 ounces (115 g) of scallops.

Storing Fish and Shellfish

At home, unwrap fish and rinse it under cool running water. Place it in a plastic container, covered with damp paper towels, and keep it in the coldest part of the refrigerator, ideally at 32° to 36°F (0° to 2°C). Cook fresh fish, shrimp, or scallops the day of purchase, if possible—never wait longer than 36 hours.

Cover live oysters, clams, and mussels with wet paper towels and refrigerate them. Don't store them in water or airtight containers or they will suffocate. Grill them as soon as possible. Cover live crabs and lobsters with wet paper towels and refrigerate them. Cook them within 12 hours. Eat fresh-cooked crab or lobster on the day you buy it or within 2 days.

For best results, freeze fresh, high-quality fish or shellfish. Wrap it airtight in heavy moistureproof freezer wrap. Seal securely and label the package. Freeze at 0°F (−18°C) or lower. Moderately fatty fish and shellfish should keep well in the freezer for up to 3 months. Leaner fish and shellfish can remain frozen up to 6 months.

Shelling, Deveining & Butterflying Shrimp

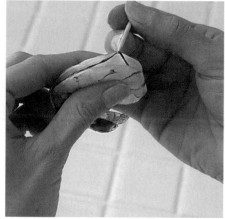

To shell raw shrimp, first pull the legs apart to a point where you can slip your fingers under the shell, then peel the shell away from the body. Consult your recipe, however; some dishes call for the tail to be left in place.

To devein shelled shrimp, use a sharp knife to cut a 1/4-inch (6-mm) slit along back. Use a small skewer or wooden pick to lift out the vein, or rinse it out under cool running water. To devein unshelled shrimp, insert a pick or skewer between shell segments and lift out the vein in several places.

To butterfly shrimp, use a sharp knife to cut more deeply along the back of the shrimp, following the vein. You will need to cut almost all the way through to make the shrimp lay flat. Remove the intestinal vein.

Preparing Lobsters for the Grill

Hold the body from the top behind the claws and plunge it headfirst into rapidly boiling water. Return water to a boil; reduce heat, cover, and simmer for 5 minutes.

Split the lobsters lengthwise cutting through the back shell. Remove and discard the stomach sac (behind head). Pull out and discard the intestinal vein, which runs to the end of the tail.

Scoop out the lobster tomalley (yellow-colored liver) and any coral-colored roe in the body cavity. Discard these materials, unless you have another purpose for them. Rinse well, then drain.

Preparing Crabs for the Grill

Holding the crab from the rear, plunge it headfirst into rapidly boiling water, being careful not to splash yourself. Return the water to a boil, then reduce the heat, cover, and simmer for 5 minutes.

To clean a crab, first break off and discard the triangular flap on the underside of crab.

Next, turn the crab over and, starting from rear, pull firmly to lift off the back of its shell.

Pull off and discard the spongy white gills from the body and the tiny paddles from the front. Scoop out the golden crab butter and reserve, if desired. Rinse the body well, then drain.

When Are Fish and Shellfish Safe to Eat?

The old axiom that oysters, clams, and mussels should only be eaten in the months containing the letter "r" no longer holds true. Nowadays, just about any shellfish can be purchased at any time, because the commercial beds are inspected regularly and have to be certified safe. A word of caution, however: If you gather your own shellfish, check with your county or state department of health to be sure that the shellfish in the area are safe

One specific type of bacteria—Vibrio vulnificus—is sometimes found in raw oysters that are harvested from the Gulf of Mexico. While not a threat to most healthy people, the bacteria can cause illness or death in people with certain medical conditions. Consult your physician. The Food and Drug Administration (FDA) advises that you cook oysters from the Gulf thoroughly before consuming them.

Unlike meat and poultry, seafood is not subject to continuous mandatory federal inspection. Your best assurance of getting seafood that's both good-tasting and safe is to buy only from a reliable, high-quality market. For additional information, call the Seafood Hotline at (800) FDA-4010.

Grilling Guide for Seafood

Type of Seafood	Thickness or Weight	Approximate Cooking Time

FILLETS, STEAKS & BONELESS CUBES FOR KEBABS

Place fish on cooking grate (support less-firm fillets on heavy-duty foil), using Direct Method for a charcoal grill, Indirect Method/Medium Heat for a gas grill. Cook for time given in chart or until fish is opaque but still moist in thickest part; turn once halfway through cooking time (unless fish is on foil).

Type of Seafood	Thickness or Weight	Approximate Cooking Time
Fillets	½ inch (1 cm)	6–8 minutes
	¾ inch (2 cm)	8–10 minutes
Fillets and steaks	1 inch (2.5 cm)	10 minutes
Boneless cubes for kebabs	1 inch (2.5 cm)	8–10 minutes

WHOLE FILLETS & WHOLE FISH

Place whole fillets and whole fish, skin side down, on cooking grate (support less-firm fish on heavy-duty foil), using Indirect Method for a charcoal grill, Indirect Method/Medium Heat for a gas grill. Cook for time given in chart or until fish is opaque but still moist in thickest part.

Type of Seafood	Thickness or Weight	Approximate Cooking Time
Whole fish fillets	1½ inches (3.5 cm)	20 minutes
Whole fish	1–1½ inches (2.5–3.5 cm)	10–15 minutes
	2–2½ inches (5–6 cm)	30–35 minutes
	3 inches (8 cm)	45 minutes

SHELLFISH

Place shellfish on cooking grate, using Direct Method for a charcoal grill, Indirect Method/Medium Heat for a gas grill. Cook crab, lobster, shrimp, and scallops for time given in chart or until opaque in thickest part; turn once halfway through cooking time. Scrub and rinse live clams, mussels, and oysters; cook them until shells open; discard any that do not open.

Type of Seafood	Thickness or Weight	Approximate Cooking Time
Crab, whole (precook for 5 minutes)	About 2½ lbs (1.15 kg)	10–12 minutes
Lobster, whole (precook for 5 minutes)	About 2 lbs (905 g)	8–10 minutes
Lobster tails	8–10 oz (230–285 g)	8 minutes
Shrimp		
large	Under 30 per lb (455 g)	4–5 minutes
colossal (also called prawns)	10–15 per lb (455 g)	6–8 minutes
extra-colossal (also called prawns)	Under 10 per lb (455 g)	8–10 minutes
Scallops	1–2 inches (2.5–5 cm) in diameter	5–8 minutes
Clams, hard-shell	Medium-size	5–8 minutes
Mussels	Under 12 per lb (455 g)	4–5 minutes
Oysters	Small	8 minutes

Fish & Shellfish Suitable for Grilling

Bass (striped bass, white bass)

Bluefish (snapper)

Buffalo

Catfish

Clams (Atlantic hard-shell, such as little necks and cherry stones; Pacific hard-shell, such as littleneck and manilas)

Cod (Atlantic cod, Pacific cod, haddock, Atlantic pollock, Alaska pollock, cusk, Atlantic whiting, Pacific whiting, white hake, red hake, hoki, Antarctic whiting or queen)

Crab (Blue, Dungeness)

Croaker (Atlantic croaker, spot)

Drum (red drum or red fish, black drum)

Halibut (Pacific halibut, Atlantic halibut)

Jack (amberjack, yellowtail, jack cravalle)

Lingcod

Lobster (American or Maine lobster, spiny or rock lobster)

Mackerel (Atlantic, Spanish, king, cero, Pacific, and Pacific jack mackerel; wahoo or ono)

Mahi mahi

Monkfish (angler, goosefish)

Mullet (striped mullet, black or jumping mullet)

Mussels (blue, New Zealand green, or green-lipped mussels)

Orange roughy

Oysters (Pacific, Olympia, Atlantic, or Eastern oysters)

Pompano (Florida pompano)

Rockfish (Atlantic and Pacific ocean perch, Pacific rockfish, often called Pacific snapper or rock cod)

Sablefish (black cod, butterfish)

Salmon (Atlantic, king or chinook, silver or coho, pink, sockeye, chum salmon)

Scallops (sea scallops, bay or Cape Cod scallops)

Sea bass/grouper (black and white sea bass, black and red grouper, Chilean sea bass, bluenose)

Sea trout/weakfish (spotted sea trout, gray weakfish)

Shad

Shark (thresher, soupfin, bonito, blacktip, mako, sandbar shark)

Shrimp ("prawns" used for very large shrimp)

Smelt (rainbow and eulachon or Columbia River smelt, grunion, silversides)

Snapper (red snapper, Florida and Caribbean snappers such as mutton and silk snappers, yellowtail, vermilion, gray)

Sturgeon

Swordfish

Tilapia

Trout (rainbow trout, steelhead trout, Arctic char, lake trout)

Tuna (albacore or tombo, bluefin, yellowfin or ahi, bigeye)

Whitefish (lake whitefish, cisco)

Testing for Doneness

As fish cooks, its translucent flesh changes to opaque pink (in the case of the salmon shown here) or white for most other types of fish.

To check for doneness, cut into the thickest part of fish. It is ready when it has just turned opaque, all the way to its center. Due to retained heat, the fish will continue to cook as you carry it to the table.

Glossary

BASTE
Seasoned liquid brushed over food as it cooks to keep surface moist and add flavor

BUTTERFLY
To make a horizontal cut through middle of a thick piece of meat, leaving about 1 inch (2.5 cm) uncut, and then opening piece out and flattening it

CARVING BOARD
Wooden board with a well for catching juices from meat as it is being carved

CHARCOAL BRIQUETS
Compact 2-inch (5-cm) pieces of fuel made of charcoal and additives; when ignited, they provide even heat for cooking

CHAR-BASKET™ FUEL HOLDERS
Hold charcoal against sides of grill to provide a larger cooking area when Indirect Method is used; charcoal rails serve the same function

COOKING GRATE
Metal grill on which food is cooked; hinged sides facilitate addition of charcoal briquets

DEGLAZE
To loosen drippings on bottom of a roasting or frying pan by stirring in wine, stock, or another liquid

DIRECT METHOD
Grilling technique, used for small or thin cuts of meat and other foods that cook in less than 25 minutes; the food is cooked directly over heat source and turned once halfway through grilling time; on a gas grill, used only for preheating and searing

DRY RUB
Highly concentrated blend of herbs and spices that is rubbed all over food before cooking to impart flavor

DRIP PAN
Foil pan placed beneath food to catch melted fat and juices when food is cooked by Indirect Method

GLAZE
To coat with a baste or sauce, so as to give a sheen to cooked food

GRIDDLE
Heavy, flat pan with a metal handle usually made of cast iron and used to cook breakfast fare, fajitas, or grilled sandwiches

GRILL BRUSH
Stiff brass bristle brush used for removing stubborn food residue from the cooking grate

GRILLING
Cooking food on a metal grate over a heat source (charcoal, gas, or electric coil)

INDIRECT METHOD
Grilling technique, used primarily for larger cuts of meat and other foods that require cooking times longer than 25 minutes; food is cooked by reflected heat (not directly above heat source), sealing in juices and eliminating the need for turning; this method can only be used with a covered grill

INSTANT-READ THERMOMETER
Type of meat thermometer that registers the internal temperature of food within seconds of being inserted; they are not safe for use in the oven

MARINADE
Seasoned liquid (usually containing an acidic ingredient, such as vinegar, wine, or citrus juice) in which food soaks, tenderizing it and enhancing flavor

SEAR
To brown meat directly above heat source at a high temperature, for just a brief time, to seal in juices

SKEWER
Thin metal or bamboo sticks of various lengths on which pieces of meat, poultry, fish, or vegetables are secured prior to grilling

SPATULA
Flat, thin tool used to turn and lift foods on the grill

TONGS
Tool used to grasp and turn foods; usually made of metal with two pieces joined at one end

WOOD CHIPS
Small chips of dried, fragrant hardwoods used to impart a smoky flavor to foods

WOOD CHUNKS
Chunks of dried, fragrant hardwoods used either as a fuel or to add smoky flavor to foods as they cook

ZEST
Thin, outermost layer of peel (colored part only) of citrus fruits

Recipes

Island Grilled Salmon

A hearty salmon fillet and fresh pineapple rings soak up a savory marinade that hints of the tropics. Strewn with toasted sesame seeds and sliced green onion, the grilled fish and fruit make an inviting platter.

Charcoal	Direct
Gas	Indirect/Medium Heat
Marinating time	30 minutes–1 hour
Grilling time	About 10 minutes

1   salmon fillet, about 2 pounds (905 g), cut about 1 inch (2.5 cm) thick

3   tablespoons *each* lime juice and Oriental sesame oil

1   tablespoon *each* brown sugar, minced fresh ginger, and soy sauce

1   medium-size pineapple, peeled, cut crosswise into 6 slices, and cored

1   teaspoon sesame seeds

1   tablespoon sliced green onion

Lime wedges

Salt

Rinse fish and pat dry. Combine lime juice, oil, sugar, ginger, and soy sauce in a large heavy-duty plastic food bag. Add salmon and pineapple and seal bag securely. Rotate bag to distribute marinade and place in a shallow pan. Refrigerate for at least 30 minutes or up to 1 hour, turning bag once.

Meanwhile, toast sesame seeds in a small frying pan over medium heat, shaking pan often, until golden (about 3 minutes). Remove from pan and set aside.

Remove fish and pineapple from bag and drain, discarding marinade. Lay fish, skin side down, on a piece of heavy-duty foil. Cut foil to follow outline of fish, leaving a 1- to 2-inch (2.5- to 5-cm) border. Crimp edges of foil to fit against fish. Arrange foil-supported fish and pineapple on cooking grate. Place lid on grill. Cook, turning pineapple once halfway through cooking time, until pineapple is browned and fish is opaque but still moist in thickest part (about 10 minutes; cut fish to test).

Supporting fish with foil and a wide metal spatula, transfer to a platter along with fruit. Sprinkle fish and fruit with sesame seeds and onion. Garnish with lime wedges. Season to taste with salt.

MAKES 6 SERVINGS.

Per serving: 353 calories (44% from fat), 17 g total fat (3 g saturated fat), 83 mg cholesterol, 242 mg sodium, 19 carbohydrates, 2 g fiber, 31 g protein, 36 mg calcium, 2 mg iron

Drunken Salmon

Scotch and salmon, anyone? You'll think the combination an instant cl__ discover how the smoky whiskey flavor complements the fish. For a fitting __ grill skewers of whole mushrooms, onion wedges, and precooked red potato__ a mixture of olive oil and sage.

Charcoal	Direct
Gas	Indirect/Medium Heat
Marinating time	1–3 hours
Grilling time	About 10 minutes

4 salmon steaks, about 1½ pounds (680 g) *total,* cut about 1 inch (2.5 cm) thick

½ teaspoon dried dill weed or dried tarragon

1 teaspoon *each* coarsely ground pepper and salad oil

2 tablespoons lemon juice

¼ cup (60 ml) Scotch or Bourbon

Lemon wedges

Salt

Very Easy

Rinse salmon and pat dry. Combine dill, pepper, oil, lemon juice, and Scotch in a large heavy-duty plastic food bag or nonreactive bowl. Add salmon and seal bag (or cover bowl). Rotate bag to distribute marinade and place in a shallow pan. Refrigerate for at least 1 hour or up to 3 hours, turning salmon occasionally.

Remove steaks from bag and drain, reserving marinade in a 1- to 1½-quart (950-ml to 1.4-liter) metal-handled pan. Arrange fish on cooking grate. Place lid on grill. Cook for 5 minutes. Turn fish with a wide metal spatula, brush with some of the reserved marinade, and set pan beside fish. Continue to cook until sauce is simmering and fish is opaque but still moist in center (about 5 more minutes; cut to test).

Using spatula, transfer fish to a platter or individual plates. Pour hot marinade over fish and garnish with lemon wedges. Season to taste with salt.

MAKES 4 SERVINGS.

Per serving: 261 calories (44% from fat), 11 g total fat (2 g saturated fat), 82 mg cholesterol, 68 mg sodium, 1 g carbohydrates, 0 g fiber, 30 g protein, 23 mg calcium, 1 mg iron

Baby Salmon with Basil Vinaigrette

Grilled baby salmon fillets rest on a bed of mesclun, a blend of salad greens that may i̶n̶c̶l̶u̶d̶e̶, among other things, arugula, frisée, radicchio, Oriental greens, and red and green lettuces. Try this dish with the fresh and crispy Corn Relish below.

Charcoal	Direct
Gas	Indirect/Medium Heat
Marinating time	1 hour or until next day
Grilling time	6–8 minutes

Basil Vinaigrette (see below)

4 baby salmon fillets, 6 to 7 ounces (170 to 200 g) *each*, cut about ½ inch (1 cm) thick

Corn Relish (see below)

8 to 10 cups (1.9 to 2.4 liters) mesclun or other mixed greens, rinsed and crisped

2 large red or yellow tomatoes, thickly sliced

Basil Vinaigrette

⅓ cup (80 ml) *each* balsamic and red wine vinegars

½ cup (120 ml) firmly packed chopped fresh basil

1 tablespoon *each* minced garlic and fresh tarragon

2 to 4 teaspoons Asian red chili paste with garlic

½ cup (120 ml) olive oil

To prepare Basil Vinaigrette, combine balsamic vinegar, red wine vinegar, basil, garlic, tarragon, and chili paste to taste in a blender or food processor. With motor running, slowly add oil. If made ahead, cover and refrigerate for up to 2 days.

Rinse salmon fillets and pat dry. Pour ¾ cup (180 ml) of the Basil Vinaigrette marinade into a large heavy-duty plastic food bag or nonreactive bowl. Add fish to bag and seal (or cover bowl). Rotate bag to distribute marinade and place in a shallow pan. Refrigerate for at least 1 hour or until next day, turning fish occasionally.

Remove fish from bag and drain, discarding marinade in bag. Arrange fish on cooking grate. Place lid on grill. Cook, turning once with a wide metal spatula halfway through cooking time, until salmon is opaque but still moist in thickest part (6 to 8 minutes; cut to test). Using spatula, remove from grill and keep warm.

Mix mesclun with ¼ cup of Basil Vinaigrette (save remaining vinaigrette for Corn Relish) and mound on individual plates. Lay fish over greens. Serve with tomato slices and Corn Relish.

MAKES 4 SERVINGS.

Per serving: 564 calories (63% from fat), 39 g total fat (6 g saturated fat), 101 mg cholesterol, 130 mg sodium, 14 g carbohydrates, 2 g fiber, 39 g protein, 135 mg calcium, 4 mg iron

Corn Relish

3 cups (710 ml) fresh corn kernels, cut from about 4 ears cooked corn

⅓ cup (80 ml) each *diced green and red bell peppers*

¼ cup (60 ml) *diced ripe olives*

½ cup (120 ml) *diced red onion*

Salt and pepper

Combine corn, bell peppers, olives, and onion in a large bowl. Stir in ⅓ cup (80 ml) of the Basil Vinaigrette. Season to taste with salt and pepper. Cover and refrigerate for at least 1 hour or until next day.

Per serving: 122 calories (14% from fat), 2 g total fat (0 g saturated fat), 0 mg cholesterol, 94 mg sodium, 25 g carbohydrates, 5 g fiber, 4 g protein, 17 mg calcium, 1 mg iron

Salads

Salads can be the perfect start, finish, or accent to any grilled meal. Clean, crisp, and refreshing, vividly colored salads of greens and fruits make attractive company for any grilled meal. They're healthy and allow you to take advantage of produce in season. As an added benefit, they can be prepared ahead.

Egg-Safe Caesar Salad

1	egg white
¼	cup (60 ml) lemon juice
⅓	cup (80 ml) olive oil
2	cloves garlic, minced or pressed
1	teaspoon coarse-grained mustard
½	teaspoon *each* Worcestershire and salt
	Pepper
1	large head romaine lettuce, rinsed and crisped
1	cup (240 ml) croutons
¼	cup (60 ml) freshly grated Parmesan cheese
5	canned anchovy fillets, drained and chopped

Combine egg white and lemon juice in an airtight container. Cover and refrigerate for at least 2 days or up to 4 days.

Place egg mixture in a food processor or blender. Add oil, garlic, mustard, Worcestershire, and salt. Whirl until blended. Season to taste with pepper.

Tear lettuce into bite-size pieces and place in a serving bowl. Add dressing and mix gently. Top with croutons, cheese, and anchovies.

MAKES 4 SERVINGS.

Per serving: 265 calories (70% from fat), 21 g total fat (4 g saturated fat), 8 mg cholesterol, 673 mg sodium, 12 g carbohydrates, 3.3 g fiber, 9 g protein, 162 mg calcium, 3 mg iron

Gorgonzola, Apple & Walnut Salad

5	tablespoons salad oil
1	teaspoon soy sauce
⅜	teaspoon salt
¼	teaspoon ground ginger
⅛	teaspoon garlic powder
1	cup (240 ml) walnut halves
¼	cup (60 ml) walnut oil
2	tablespoons *each* white wine vinegar and lemon juice
2	teaspoons Dijon mustard
	Dash of ground white pepper
2	large tart green apples
1	large head romaine or green leaf lettuce, rinsed and crisped
3	ounces (85 g) crumbled Gorgonzola cheese

In an 8-inch (20-cm) square baking pan, combine 1 tablespoon of the salad oil, soy sauce, ¼ teaspoon of the salt, ginger, and garlic powder. Add walnuts and stir to coat. Spread nuts in a single layer. Bake in a 250°F (120°C) oven, stirring occasionally, until crisp and browned (about 30 minutes). Let cool on paper towels. If made ahead, store airtight at room temperature for up to 1 week.

In a small bowl, combine remaining salad oil, walnut oil, vinegar, lemon juice, mustard, pepper, and remaining salt; blend well and set aside. Core and thinly slice apples. Tear lettuce into bite-size pieces. Combine lettuce and apples in a serving bowl. Mix dressing again and pour over salad. Mix gently. Sprinkle with walnuts and cheese.

MAKES 6 TO 8 SERVINGS.

Per serving: 345 calories (77% from fat), 31 g total fat (5 g saturated fat), 11 mg cholesterol, 377 mg sodium, 15 g carbohydrates, 4 g fiber, 6 g protein, 118 mg calcium, 2 mg iron

Orange & Onion Salad

1	small avocado
¼	cup (60 ml) *each* sour cream and lemon juice
⅛	teaspoon ground red pepper (cayenne)
2	large oranges
2	thin slices red onion
1	cup (240 ml) firmly packed alfalfa sprouts
1	cup (240 ml) thinly sliced cucumber

Pit and peel avocado. Place in a blender or food processor; add sour cream, lemon juice, and ground red pepper. Whirl until smooth. If made ahead, cover and refrigerate dressing until next day.

Cut peel and white membrane from oranges. Slice oranges crosswise ¼ inch (6 mm) thick. Cut onion slices in half crosswise; separate into strips.

Spread alfalfa sprouts on individual plates. Overlap orange and cucumber slices over sprouts. Spoon on dressing and garnish with onion.

MAKES 4 SERVINGS.

Per serving: 136 calories (46% from fat), 8 g total fat (3 g saturated fat), 6 mg cholesterol, 15 mg sodium, 17 g carbohydrates, 4 g fiber, 2 g protein, 76 mg calcium, 1 mg iron

Three-Mustard Salad

¼	cup (60 ml) salad oil
2	tablespoons *each* mustard seeds, white wine vinegar, and Dijon mustard
2	teaspoons dried mustard
½	to 1 teaspoon liquid hot pepper seasoning
1	*each* medium-size cucumber, green bell pepper, and red onion
4	large tomatoes
	Salt and pepper

In a small bowl, combine oil, mustard seeds, vinegar, Dijon mustard, dried mustard, and hot pepper seasoning to taste; set aside.

Score cucumber skin lengthwise with a fork, or peel; slice about ¼ inch (6 mm) thick. Cut bell pepper in half lengthwise and discard seeds; slice crosswise ¼ inch (6 mm) thick. Thinly slice onion and separate into rings. Cut tomatoes into wedges about ½ inch (1 cm) thick.

In a serving bowl, combine cucumber, bell pepper, onion, and tomatoes. Add dressing and mix gently. Season to taste with salt and pepper.

MAKES 6 TO 8 SERVINGS.

Per serving: 147 calories (56% from fat), 10 g total fat (1 g saturated fat), 0 mg cholesterol, 136 mg sodium, 14 g carbohydrates, 3 g fiber, 3 g protein, 41 mg calcium, 1 mg iron

Very Easy

Salad Greens

You'll find a wonderful variety of greens available in markets today. For a change of pace, try some of these.

- **Arugula (rocket, roquette).** *The bright green leaves of arugula have a spicy, mustardy tang.*

- **Baby bok choy.** *Harvested young, baby bok choy is a milder-flavored version of the mature green, which has a cabbagelike taste.*

- **Baby chicory (frisée).** *More softly textured than mature chicory, baby chicory tastes subtly bitter.*

- **Napa cabbage (celery cabbage, Chinese cabbage).** *A bit sweeter than more familiar cabbages, napa cabbage has a moist crispness and a slightly zesty flavor.*

- **Radicchio (red chicory, Italian red lettuce).** *Small, round, or elongated heads of radicchio taste somewhat like escarole; the sturdy leaves range from purplish red to variegated red and green.*

- **Red oak-leaf lettuce.** *Most of the leaves of this tender, mild-tasting lettuce are so small you can use them whole.*

Salmon on Wilted Chicory Salad

With its rosy hue, salmon looks wonderful on a bed of glossy greens.
This dish needs nothing more in the way of accompaniment than a loaf of crusty bread.

Charcoal	Direct
Gas	Indirect/Medium Heat
Grilling time	About 10 minutes

½ cup (120 ml) extra-virgin
    olive oil

8   ounces (230 g) chanterelles
    or regular button
    mushrooms, cut into about
    ½-inch (1-cm) pieces

¼   cup (60 ml) thinly sliced
    green onions

2   tablespoons vinegar

4   cloves garlic, minced
    or pressed

⅓   cup (80 ml) minced fresh
    thyme or 2 tablespoons
    dried thyme

9   cups (2.2 liters) bite-size
    pieces chicory (curly endive),
    rinsed and crisped

6   salmon or rockfish steaks
    or fillets, about 2½ pounds
    (1.15 kg) *total*, cut about
    1 inch (2.5 cm) thick

    Salt and pepper

Heat 2 tablespoons of the oil in a wide frying pan over medium-high heat. Add chanterelles and cook, stirring occasionally, until lightly browned (10 to 12 minutes). Stir in ¼ cup (60 ml) more oil. Add onions, vinegar, garlic, and half the thyme; stir well. Remove from heat and add chicory (half at a time, if necessary), turning until well coated. Mound salad on individual plates and set aside.

Rinse salmon and pat dry. Brush all over with remaining 2 tablespoons oil; sprinkle with remaining thyme. Arrange fish on cooking grate. Place lid on grill. Cook, turning once with a wide metal spatula halfway through cooking time, until fish is opaque but still moist in thickest part (about 10 minutes; cut to test). Using spatula, place a fish steak on each salad. Season to taste with salt and pepper.

MAKES 6 SERVINGS.

Per serving: 476 calories (55% from fat), 30 g total fat (5 g saturated fat), 92 mg cholesterol, 198 mg sodium, 16 g carbohydrates, 5 g fiber, 39 g protein, 326 mg calcium, 6 mg iron

GRILL BY THE BOOK
TIP

To make grilled toast, brush thick slices of crusty French bread with olive oil (flavored or plain) or melted butter. Lay the bread on the cooking grate and cook, turning once, until lightly toasted on both sides.

Salmon with Potato & Watercress Salad

*This savory, dark-glazed salmon is grilled with a little bit of added smoke. Its companion dish—
a potato salad with crisp green onions and peppery watercress—makes the meal complete.*

Charcoal	Direct
Gas	Indirect/Medium Heat
Grilling time	About 20 minutes

3 pounds (1.35 kg) small red thin-skinned potatoes, about 2 inches (5 cm) in diameter

About 2 cups (470 ml) alder, mesquite, or hickory wood chips

1 cup (240 ml) thinly sliced green onions

1 cup (240 ml) seasoned rice vinegar; or 1 cup (240 ml) distilled white vinegar and 1 tablespoon sugar

About 8 ounces (230 g) watercress, rinsed and crisped

1 salmon fillet, about 2 pounds (905 g), cut about 1½ inches (3.5 cm) thick

1 tablespoon *each* brown sugar and soy sauce

Lowfat

In a 5- to 6-quart (5- to 6-liter) pan, bring 2 quarts (1.9 liters) water to a boil over high heat. Add potatoes; reduce heat, cover, and simmer until tender when pierced (about 20 minutes). Drain, immerse in cold water, and drain again. (At this point, you may cover and refrigerate until next day.)

Place wood chips in a large bowl. Add warm water to make them float; let soak for 30 minutes. Place onions in another bowl. Add cold water to cover; let soak for 15 minutes. Drain well; return to bowl and mix with vinegar. Cut potatoes into quarters and add to onions. Cut stems from watercress sprigs. Finely chop enough of the stems to make ½ cup (120 ml); reserve remainder for other uses. Stir chopped stems into potato mixture. Mound watercress sprigs and potato salad on a side of a platter; cover and refrigerate.

Rinse fish and pat dry. Place, skin side down, on a piece of lightly oiled heavy-duty foil. Cut foil along outline of fish, leaving about a 1- to 2-inch (2.5- to 5-cm) border. Crimp edges of foil to fit against fish. In a small bowl, combine brown sugar and soy sauce; brush all over fish.

In a charcoal barbecue, drain chips; scatter equally onto each mound of coals. *In a gas barbecue,* place chips in a foil pan and set under cooking grate on top of heat source in left front corner of barbecue; turn heat to High and preheat for 10 to 15 minutes. Then turn heat to Indirect/Medium. Set salmon in center of cooking grate. Place lid on grill. Cook until fish is opaque but still moist in thickest part (about 20 minutes; cut to test). Transfer to platter.

MAKES 6 SERVINGS.

Per serving: 450 calories (20% from fat), 10 g total fat (1 g saturated fat), 83 mg cholesterol, 1065 mg sodium, 53 g carbohydrates, 5 g fiber, 36 g protein, 74 mg calcium, 3 mg iron

Tuna with Mint-Mango Chutney

The fresh chutney that accompanies these thick tuna steaks brings together mango, mint, citrus, ginger, and chiles.

Charcoal	Direct
Gas	Indirect/Medium Heat
Marinating time	15 minutes–2 hours
Grilling time	About 10 minutes

¼ cup (60 ml) *each* chopped fresh mint and orange juice

2 tablespoons lime juice

1 tablespoon minced fresh ginger

⅛ to ¼ teaspoon minced, seeded fresh habanero chile or 1 to 2 teaspoons minced, seeded fresh serrano chile

4 tuna steaks, such as yellowfin (ahi), albacore (tombo), or bluefin, 4 to 6 ounces (115 to 170 g) *each,* cut about 1 inch (2.5 cm) thick

1 large firm-ripe mango

Mint sprigs

Salt and pepper

Combine chopped mint, orange juice, lime juice, ginger, and chile to taste in a large bowl. Pour about a third of the mint mixture into a large heavy-duty plastic food bag or nonreactive bowl; set remaining mixture aside. Rinse fish and pat dry. Add to bag and seal (or cover bowl). Rotate bag to distribute marinade and place in a shallow pan. Refrigerate for at least 15 minutes or up to 2 hours, turning fish occasionally.

Meanwhile, peel mango. Slice fruit off each side and from edges of wide flat pit. Cut into ½ inch (1 cm) cubes. Stir into reserved mint mixture; set aside.

Remove fish from bag and drain, discarding marinade in bag. Arrange fish on cooking grate. Place lid on grill. Cook, turning once with a wide metal spatula halfway through cooking time, until fish is opaque but still moist in center (about 10 minutes; cut to test). Using spatula, transfer to a platter or individual plates and top with mango mixture. Garnish with mint sprigs. Season to taste with salt and pepper.

MAKES 4 SERVINGS.

Per serving: 243 calories (24% from fat), 6 g total fat (2 g saturated fat), 48 mg cholesterol, 52 mg sodium, 16 g carbohydrates, 1 g fiber, 30 g protein, 12 mg calcium, 2 mg iron

Tuna with Four Sauce Variations

Experiment with a range of sauces and flavored butters for the tuna that you grill. There are red-fleshed varieties of this delectable fish called bluefin and yellowfin; the latter is often referred to as ahi. There is also a cream-colored variety called albacore, or tombo. Availability may vary with the season.

Charcoal	Direct
Gas	Indirect/Medium Heat
Grilling time	About 10 minutes

Sauce of your choice (see below)

4   tuna steaks, such as yellowfin (ahi), albacore (tombo), or bluefin, about 1 pound (455 g) *total*, cut about 1 inch (2.5 cm) thick

About 2 tablespoons olive oil or salad oil

Salt and pepper

Very Easy

Tuna Steak with Lime Butter Sauce

Prepare sauce of your choice. If made ahead, cover and refrigerate until next day; if necessary, reheat before using.

Rinse fish and pat dry. Brush all over with oil. Arrange on cooking grate. Place lid on grill. Cook, turning once with a wide metal spatula halfway through cooking time, until fish is opaque but still moist in center (about 10 minutes; cut to test). Season to taste with salt and pepper. Serve with sauce.

MAKES 4 SERVINGS.

Per serving: 223 calories (51% from fat), 12 g total fat (2 g saturated fat), 43 mg cholesterol, 44 mg sodium, 0 g carbohydrates, 0 g fiber, 26 g protein, 0 mg calcium, 1 mg iron

Teriyaki Sauce with Papaya

In a 2- to 3-quart (1.9- to 2.8-liter) pan, boil soy sauce, sugar, sake, and fresh ginger over high heat, stirring, until reduced to about ⅓ cup (80 ml). Discard ginger slices. Keep warm.

To serve, spoon sauce over fish. Top with papaya and candied ginger. Arrange bell pepper alongside.

MAKES 4 SERVINGS.

Per serving: 115 calories (1% from fat), 0 g total fat (0 g saturated fat), 0 mg cholesterol, 1 mg sodium, 22 g carbohydrates, 1 g fiber, 1 g protein, 15 mg calcium, 1 mg iron

¼   cup (60 ml) soy sauce

¼   cup (50 g) sugar

6   tablespoons sake or dry sherry

3   thin slices fresh ginger

8   to 12 thin slices peeled firm-ripe papaya or mango

2   teaspoons chopped candied or crystallized ginger

1   medium-size green bell pepper, cut into thin slivers

Oregano-Chili Butter

¼	cup (60 ml) butter or margarine, at room temperature
2	teaspoons chili powder
2	teaspoons chopped fresh oregano or ¾ teaspoon dried oregano
4	oregano or watercress sprigs

In a small bowl, beat butter, chili powder, and chopped oregano until fluffy. Cover and let stand for up to 30 minutes.

To serve, top each steak with a pat of the butter mixture and garnish with oregano sprigs.

MAKES 4 SERVINGS.

Per serving: 107 calories (96% from fat), 12 g total fat (7 g saturated fat), 31 mg cholesterol, 130 mg sodium, 1 g carbohydrates, 0 g fiber, 0 g protein, 13 mg calcium, 0 mg iron

South-of-the-Border Sauce

1	medium-size tomato, chopped
¼	cup (60 ml) chopped green bell pepper
2	tablespoons *each* chopped radish and green onion
1	tablespoon *each* chopped cilantro and canned diced green chiles
4	cilantro sprigs
1	cup (240 ml) matchstick pieces jicama
	Tortilla chips

In a small bowl, combine tomato, bell pepper, radish, onion, chopped cilantro, and chiles. Cover and let stand for up to 30 minutes.

To serve, spoon sauce over fish and garnish with cilantro sprigs. Accompany with jicama and tortilla chips.

MAKES 4 SERVINGS.

Per serving: 23 calories (6% from fat), 0 g total fat (0 g saturated fat), 0 mg cholesterol, 7 mg sodium, 5 g carbohydrates, 1 g fiber, 1 g protein, 11 mg calcium, 0 mg iron

Lime Butter Sauce

¼	cup (60 ml) butter or margarine, at room temperature
1	teaspoon grated lime zest
1	tablespoon lime juice
	Thinly sliced lime
	Parsley sprigs

In a small bowl, beat butter, lime zest, and lime juice until fluffy. Cover and let stand for up to 30 minutes.

To serve, top each steak with a pat of the butter mixture. Garnish with lime slices and parsley.

MAKES 4 SERVINGS.

Per serving: 34 calories (98% from fat), 4 g total fat (10 g saturated fat), 10 mg cholesterol, 39 mg sodium, 0 g carbohydrates, 0 g fiber, 0 g protein, 2 mg calcium, 0 mg iron

Tuna Loin with Basil & Cucumbers

A cucumber salad with basil and Parmesan accompanies this marinated tuna loin.

Charcoal	Direct
Gas	Indirect/Medium Heat
Marinating time	3-6 hours
Grilling time	20–25 minutes

¾ cup (180 ml) lightly packed fresh basil; or 3 tablespoons dried basil and ¼ cup (60 ml) lightly packed parsley sprigs

½ cup (120 ml) *each* salad oil and white wine vinegar

¼ cup (60 ml) freshly grated Parmesan cheese

3 cloves garlic

¼ teaspoon pepper

1 boneless skinned or unskinned tuna loin, such as yellowfin (ahi), albacore (tombo), or bluefin, about 2 pounds (905 g), cut about 2 inches (5 cm) thick

1 medium-size cucumber, peeled

Salt

In a food processor or blender, whirl basil, oil, vinegar, cheese, garlic, and pepper until smooth. Pour about two-thirds of the marinade into a large heavy-duty plastic food bag; set aside remaining marinade in a large bowl. Rinse fish and pat dry. Add to bag and seal securely. Rotate bag to distribute marinade and place in a shallow pan. Refrigerate for at least 3 hours or up to 6 hours, turning bag occasionally.

Meanwhile, cut cucumber in half lengthwise. Scoop out and discard seeds. Slice thinly and mix with remaining marinade in bowl. Cover and refrigerate for at least 3 hours or up to 6 hours.

Remove fish from bag, reserving marinade. Set on cooking grate. Place lid on grill. Cook, turning once with a wide metal spatula and brushing with reserved marinade, until fish is opaque but still moist in thickest part (20 to 25 minutes; cut to test). Using spatula, transfer fish to a board and cut crosswise into 1-inch (2.5-cm) slices. Arrange cucumber and fish on individual plates. Season to taste with salt.

MAKES 5 OR 6 SERVINGS.

Per serving: 359 calories (53% from fat), 21 g total fat (3 g saturated fat), 71 mg cholesterol, 136 mg sodium, 4 g carbohydrates, 0 g fiber, 38 g protein, 139 mg calcium, 2 mg iron

Like Mexico's popular salsa cruda, made with fresh tomatoes, onions, chiles, and lime, these three variations are light and refreshing, thanks to a wash of citrus and little or no oil. Spoon them over fish with the same abandon as you would a squeeze of lemon juice. They'll keep in the refrigerator up to 1 week.

Cucumber-Ginger Salsa

1	large cucumber
1	small red bell pepper
½	small onion
1	small fresh jalapeño chile
1	tablespoon minced cilantro
1	teaspoon minced fresh ginger
¼	cup (60 ml) lime juice
1	tablespoon Oriental sesame oil
1½	teaspoons sugar
	Salt

Seed and dice cucumber, bell pepper, and onion. Seed and mince chile. In a small nonreactive bowl, combine cucumber, bell pepper, onion, chile, cilantro, ginger, lime juice, oil, and sugar. Season to taste with salt.

MAKES ABOUT 2½ CUPS (590 ML).

Per ¼ cup (60 ml): 23 calories (52% from fat), 1 g total fat (0 g saturated fat), 0 mg cholesterol, 2 mg sodium, 3 g carbohydrates, 0 g fiber, 0 g protein, 5 mg calcium, 0 mg iron

Black Bean Salsa

1	can, about 15 ounces (425 g), cooked black beans
2	ounces (55g) smoked ham
1	small red bell pepper
½	small onion
1	small fresh jalapeño chile
⅓	cup (80 ml) lime juice
3	tablespoons minced cilantro
2	cloves garlic, minced or pressed
½	teaspoon dried mustard
	Salt and pepper

Drain beans, rinse under cool running water, and drain again. Dice ham; seed and dice bell pepper and onion. Seed and mince chile. In a large nonreactive bowl, combine beans, ham, bell pepper, onion, chile, lime juice, cilantro, garlic, and mustard. Season to taste with salt and pepper.

MAKES ABOUT 3 CUPS (710 ML).

Per ½ cup (120 ml): 66 calories (10% from fat), 1 g total fat (0 g saturated fat), 2 mg cholesterol, 129 mg sodium, 5 g carbohydrates, 1 g fiber, 2 g protein, 11 mg calcium, 0 mg iron

Orange & Radish Salsa

3	oranges
1	small fresh jalapeño chile
3	tablespoons lime juice
1	tablespoon minced cilantro
8	medium-size radishes
	Salt

Peel oranges. Holding oranges over a large nonreactive bowl, cut fruit segments from membrane and squeeze juice into bowl; discard membrane. Chop fruit. Seed and mince chile; add chile, lime juice, and cilantro. Slice radishes; cut into narrow strips so each piece is tipped in red. Just before serving, stir in radishes. Season to taste with salt.

MAKES ABOUT 3 CUPS (710 ML).

Per ¼ cup (60 ml): 21 calories (3% from fat), 0 g total fat (0 g saturated fat), 0 mg cholesterol, 1 mg sodium, 5 g carbohydrates, 1 g fiber, 0 g protein, 19 mg calcium, 0 mg iron

Swordfish with Fruit & Citrus Vinegar

Green cilantro, orange mango, and glistening blackberries top white slabs of swordfish to make this dish as colorful as it is delicious.

Charcoal	Direct
Gas	Indirect/Medium Heat
Grilling time	About 10 minutes

1½ pounds (680 g) swordfish, Pacific halibut, or sturgeon steaks, cut about 1 inch (2.5 cm) thick

1 tablespoon salad oil

1 cup (240 ml) chopped firm-ripe mango

1 cup (240 ml) blackberries, rinsed and drained

2 tablespoons chopped cilantro

¾ cup (180 ml) grapefruit, other fruit, or chili vinegar

Salt and pepper

Very Easy

Rinse fish and pat dry. Brush all over with oil. Arrange fish on cooking grate. Place lid on grill. Cook, turning once with a wide metal spatula halfway through cooking time, until fish is opaque but still moist in center (about 10 minutes; cut to test).

Using spatula, place fish on individual plates. Top with mango, blackberries, and cilantro; sprinkle with ½ cup (120 ml) of the vinegar. Season to taste with salt, pepper, and remaining vinegar.

MAKES 4 SERVINGS.

Per serving: 290 calories (32% from fat), 10 g total fat (2 g saturated fat), 66 mg cholesterol, 155 mg sodium, 15 g carbohydrates, 2 g fiber, 34 g protein, 27 mg calcium, 2 mg iron

GRILL BY THE BOOK
T I P

To make your own citrus vinegar, add peel to white vinegar, bring just to a boil, cool, and pour into a bottle. Let stand at least 1 day.

Swordfish with Rosemary Aioli

Prepare the rosemary-spiked garlic mayonnaise a day or two in advance so the flavors have time to blend. The aioli is equally good with such side dishes as sliced tomatoes and cooked small potatoes or green beans.

Charcoal	Direct
Gas	Indirect/Medium Heat
Grilling time	About 10 minutes

¾   cup (180 ml) mayonnaise

1   tablespoon lemon juice

3   cloves garlic, minced
or pressed

1   teaspoon minced fresh
rosemary or ½ teaspoon
crumbled dried rosemary

4   swordfish steaks, about
1½ pounds (680 g) *total,*
cut about 1 inch (2.5 cm)
thick

2   teaspoons olive oil

Salt

Very Easy

In a small bowl, combine mayonnaise, lemon juice, garlic, and rosemary. Cover and refrigerate aioli until ready to use or for up to 2 days.

Rinse fish and pat dry. Brush all over with oil. Arrange fish on cooking grate. Place lid on grill. Cook, turning once with a wide metal spatula halfway through cooking time, until fish is opaque but still moist in center (about 10 minutes; cut to test). Using spatula, transfer fish to a platter or individual plates. Serve with aioli. Season to taste with salt.

MAKES 4 SERVINGS.

Per serving: 504 calories (74% from fat), 41 g total fat (7 g saturated fat), 84 mg cholesterol, 373 mg sodium, 2 g carbohydrates, 0 g fiber, 31 g protein, 20 mg calcium, 1 mg iron

Shark Picante

Lime juice and ready-made salsa combine to make an easy marinade that complements the full flavor of shark. If you like, serve the fish with skewers of grilled vegetables basted with a bit of the citrus butter.

Charcoal	Direct
Gas	Indirect/Medium Heat
Marinating time	30 minutes–2 hours
Grilling time	About 10 minutes

Lime Butter (see below)

4	shark or salmon steaks, 6 to 8 ounces (170 to 230 g) *each*, cut about 1 inch (2.5 cm) thick
2	tablespoons lime juice
½	cup (120 ml) mild salsa
2	tablespoons butter or margarine, melted
	Lime wedges
	Cilantro sprigs

Lime Butter

⅓	cup (80 ml) butter or margarine, at room temperature
½	teaspoon grated lime zest
2	tablespoons lime juice
1	tablespoon minced cilantro
¼	teaspoon crushed red pepper flakes

Very Easy

In a small bowl, combine ingredients for Lime Butter. Beat until fluffy. Cover and refrigerate until ready to use or for up to 2 days.

Rinse fish and pat dry. Combine lime juice and salsa in a large heavy-duty plastic food bag or nonreactive bowl. Add fish and seal bag (or cover bowl). Rotate bag to distribute marinade and place in a shallow pan. Refrigerate for at least 30 minutes or up to 2 hours, turning fish occasionally.

Remove fish from bag and drain, discarding marinade. Brush all over with butter. Arrange fish on cooking grate. Place lid on grill. Cook, turning once with a wide metal spatula halfway through cooking time, until fish is opaque but still moist in center (about 10 minutes; cut to test).

Using spatula, transfer fish to a platter or individual plates. Spoon 2 teaspoons of the lime butter mixture onto each steak. Garnish with lime wedges and cilantro sprigs. Serve with remaining butter mixture.

MAKES 4 SERVINGS.

Per serving: 326 calories (52% from fat), 18 g total fat (8 g saturated fat), 117 mg cholesterol, 406 mg sodium, 2 g carbohydrates, 0 g fiber, 37 g protein, 64 mg calcium, 1 mg iron

Soy-Lemon Halibut

A ginger-spiked marinade adds lots of extra flavor but very few calories to naturally low-calorie grilled halibut.

Charcoal	Direct
Gas	Indirect/Medium Heat
Marinating time	1–2 hours
Grilling time	8–10 minutes

2   pounds (905 g) halibut, shark, or sea bass steaks or fillets, cut ¾ to 1 inch (2 to 2.5 cm) thick

2   tablespoons butter or margarine, melted

3   tablespoons reduced-sodium soy sauce

2   tablespoons lemon juice

1   tablespoon *each* sugar, minced fresh ginger, and Worcestershire

1   clove garlic, minced or pressed

⅛   teaspoon pepper

     Lemon wedges

Lowfat

Rinse fish and pat dry. Combine butter, soy sauce, lemon juice, sugar, ginger, Worcestershire, garlic, and pepper in a large heavy-duty plastic food bag or nonreactive bowl. Add fish and seal bag (or cover bowl). Rotate bag to distribute marinade and place in a shallow pan. Refrigerate for at least 1 hour or up 2 hours, turning fish occasionally.

Remove fish from bag and drain, reserving marinade. Arrange fish on cooking grate. Place lid on grill. Cook, turning once with a wide metal spatula and brushing with reserved marinade halfway through cooking time, until fish is opaque but still moist in thickest part (8 to 10 minutes; cut to test). Serve with lemon wedges.

MAKES 6 SERVINGS.

Per serving: 192 calories (26% from fat), 5 g total fat (2 g saturated fat), 54 mg cholesterol, 266 mg sodium, 2 g carbohydrates, 0 g fiber, 32 g protein, 73 mg calcium, 1 mg iron

Halibut Piccata

This updated version of a popular restaurant menu item is made with grilled fish instead of the traditional sautéed veal.
The white wine and caper sauce cooks in minutes and is equally delicious with any grilled fish.

Charcoal	Direct
Gas	Indirect/Medium Heat
Grilling time	8–10 minutes

1½	tablespoons olive oil
1	large clove garlic, minced or pressed
½	cup (120 ml) dry white wine
3	tablespoons lemon juice
2	tablespoons drained canned capers
1½	pounds (680 g) halibut fillets, cut about ¾ inch (2 cm) thick
	Pepper
½	cup (120 ml) finely shredded Parmesan cheese

Very Easy

Heat ½ tablespoon of the oil in a small frying pan over medium heat. Add garlic and cook, stirring, until soft (about 1 minute). Add wine, lemon juice, and capers. Boil over high heat, stirring, until reduced to about ½ cup/120 ml (3 to 5 minutes). Remove from heat and keep warm.

Rinse fish, pat dry, and cut into 4 equal-size portions. Brush with remaining oil and sprinkle lightly with pepper. Arrange fish on cooking grate. Place lid on grill. Cook, turning once with a wide metal spatula and sprinkling with cheese halfway through cooking time, until fish is opaque but still moist in thickest part (8 to 10 minutes; cut to test). Using spatula, transfer fish to a platter or individual plates. Spoon warm caper sauce over fish.

MAKES 4 SERVINGS.

Per serving: 341 calories (46% from fat), 16 g total fat (4 g saturated fat), 64 mg cholesterol, 433 mg sodium, 2 g carbohydrates, 0 g fiber, 41 g protein, 254 mg calcium, 2 mg iron

Lingcod with Mint Relish

Chile and garlic add lively accents to this refreshing, minty relish. It makes a memorable accompaniment for grilled cod, rockfish, or any other mild-flavored fish.

Charcoal	Direct
Gas	Indirect/Medium Heat
Grilling time	About 10 minutes

½   cup (120 ml) *each* fresh mint and cilantro

3   tablespoons lemon juice

1   fresh jalapeño chile, seeded and chopped

1   clove garlic

½   teaspoon ground cumin

½   cup (120 ml) sweetened shredded coconut

2   pounds (905 g) boned and skinned lingcod or rockfish fillets, *each* about 1 inch thick

     Mint sprigs

     Salt

Very Easy

In a blender or food processor, whirl the ½ cup (120 ml) mint, cilantro, lemon juice, chile, garlic, cumin, and 1 tablespoon water until smooth. Stir in coconut and set aside.

Rinse fish and pat dry. Cut into 6 equal-size pieces. Arrange on cooking grate. Place lid on grill. Cook, turning once with a wide metal spatula halfway through cooking time, until fish is opaque but still moist in thickest part (about 10 minutes; cut to test). Using spatula, transfer fish to a platter or individual plates and top with mint mixture. Garnish with mint sprigs. Season to taste with salt.

MAKES 6 SERVINGS.

Per serving: 167 calories (21% from fat), 4 g total fat (2 g saturated fat), 81 mg cholesterol, 110 mg sodium, 4 g carbohydrates, 0 g fiber, 28 g protein, 30 mg calcium, 1 mg iron

Marinades, Bastes & Sauces for Seafood

You can add flavor and moisture to barbecued fish and shellfish with a marinade, baste, or sauce. Delicate-tasting types of seafood benefit from a simple baste or sauce. The same treatment is fine for stronger-flavored fish and shellfish, but those also take well to more assertive seasoning mixtures.

Basil-Parmesan Marinade for Fish

⅔ cup (160 ml) chopped fresh basil

⅓ cup (80 ml) white wine vinegar

¼ cup (60 ml) olive oil or salad oil

3 tablespoons grated Parmesan cheese

2 cloves garlic

⅛ teaspoon pepper

In a food processor or blender, combine basil, vinegar, oil, Parmesan, garlic, and pepper. Whirl until puréed. Marinate fish in basil mixture for 20 to 30 minutes, turning fish often. Remove fish, reserving marinade. Brush marinade all over fish while it cooks.

MAKES ABOUT 1¼ CUPS (300 ML), ENOUGH FOR 4 TO 6 SERVINGS.

Per serving: 122 calories (86% from fat), 12 g total fat (2 g saturated fat), 3 mg cholesterol, 69 mg sodium, 3 g carbohydrates, 0 g fiber, 2 g protein, 104 mg calcium, 1 mg iron

Lemon-Tarragon Butter Baste for Seafood

¼ cup (60 ml) butter or margarine, melted

¼ cup (60 ml) lemon juice, dry sherry, or dry vermouth

1 tablespoon Dijon mustard

1 teaspoon dried tarragon

In a small bowl, combine butter, lemon juice, mustard, and tarragon. Brush butter mixture all over seafood while it cooks.

MAKES ABOUT ½ CUP (120 ML), ENOUGH FOR 4 TO 6 SERVINGS.

Per serving: 88 calories (95% from fat), 9 g total fat (6 g saturated fat), 25 mg cholesterol, 168 mg sodium, 1 g carbohydrates, 0 g fiber, 0 g protein, 8 mg calcium, 0 mg iron

Classic Tartar Sauce for Fish

¼ cup (60 ml) *each* mayonnaise, sour cream, and well-drained sweet pickle relish

1 tablespoon finely chopped green onion

½ teaspoon *each* lemon juice and Worcestershire

4 drops liquid hot pepper seasoning

In a small bowl, combine mayonnaise, sour cream, relish, onion, lemon juice, Worcestershire, and hot pepper seasoning. Cover and refrigerate for at least 30 minutes to blend flavors. Serve with grilled fish.

MAKES ABOUT ¾ CUP (180 ML), ENOUGH FOR 4 TO 6 SERVINGS.

Per serving: 121 calories (81% from fat), 11 g total fat (3 g saturated fat), 12 mg cholesterol, 164 mg sodium, 5 g carbohydrates, 0 g fiber, 1 g protein, 19 mg calcium, 0 mg iron

Tart Dipping Sauce for Shellfish

¼ cup (60 ml) *each* dry white wine and white wine vinegar

1 tablespoon *each* minced shallot and chives

¼ teaspoon pepper

In a small bowl, combine wine, vinegar, shallot, chives, and pepper. Serve with grilled shellfish.

MAKES ABOUT ½ CUP (120 ML), ENOUGH FOR 4 TO 6 SERVINGS .

Per serving: 11 calories (0% from fat), 0 g total fat (0 g saturated fat), 0 mg cholesterol, 1 mg sodium, 1 g carbohydrates, 0 g fiber, 1 g protein, 3 mg calcium, 1 mg iron

Striped Bass with Onion Barbecue Sauce

A delicate hint of smokiness is an excellent flavor enhancer for this moist, mild-flavored striped bass. The fish is basted with a spicy tomato marinade while it grills.

Charcoal	Direct
Gas	Indirect/Medium Heat
Grilling time	About 10 minutes

2	teaspoons olive oil
1	small onion, chopped
6	tablespoons catsup
3	tablespoons lemon juice
1½	tablespoons *each* sugar and Worcestershire
1	tablespoon prepared mustard
¼	teaspoon pepper
	Salt
2	pounds (905 g) boneless striped bass fillets, cut about 1 inch (2.5 cm) thick

Lowfat

Heat oil in a 1- to 1½-quart (950-ml to 1.4-liter) metal-handled pan over medium-high heat. Add onion and cook, stirring often, until onion begins to brown (8 to 10 minutes). Stir in catsup, lemon juice, sugar, Worcestershire, mustard, and pepper. Reduce heat and simmer, stirring occasionally, until sauce is thickened (about 10 minutes). Remove from heat and season to taste with salt.

Rinse fish and pat dry. Arrange fish, skin side down, on cooking grate and brush with some of the sauce. Place lid on grill. Cook for 5 minutes. Turn fish with a wide metal spatula, brush with more sauce, and place pan with sauce on cooking grate. Continue to cook until sauce is simmering and fish is opaque but still moist in thickest part (about 5 more minutes; cut to test).

Using spatula, transfer fish, skin side down, to a platter. Slide spatula between skin and flesh and lift off each portion. Serve with sauce.

MAKES 6 SERVINGS.

Per serving: 301 calories (24% from fat), 8 g total fat (1 g saturated fat), 182 mg cholesterol, 537 mg sodium, 15 g carbohydrates, 1 g fiber, 41 g protein, 14 mg calcium, 2 mg iron

Trout with Citrus Salsa & Jalapeño Mayonnaise

This tempting trout dish brings a range of flavors to the palate: an herbed marinade, a terrific citrus salsa, and a creamy, lime-brightened chile mayonnaise.

Charcoal	Indirect
Gas	Indirect/Medium Heat
Marinating time	1–2 hours
Grilling time	10–12 minutes

Jalapeño Mayonnaise
(see below)

4   whole trout, about 8 ounces (230 g) *each*, cleaned

¼   cup (60 ml) *each* salad oil and white wine vinegar

1½   teaspoons minced fresh basil or ½ teaspoon dried basil

1½   teaspoons minced fresh oregano or ½ teaspoon dried oregano

1   clove garlic, minced or pressed

¼   teaspoon *each* salt and pepper

Citrus Salsa (see below)

Jalapeño Mayonnaise

¾   cup (180 ml) mayonnaise

2   or 3 fresh jalapeño chiles, seeded and minced

1   clove garlic

½   teaspoon grated lime zest

1½   tablespoons lime juice

Salt

Citrus Salsa

1   large orange

1   small grapefruit

1   medium-size tomato, chopped

1   tablespoon *each* lime juice and orange juice

2   tablespoons chopped cilantro

½   teaspoon sugar

Salt

To prepare Jalapeño Mayonnaise, combine mayonnaise, chiles to taste, garlic, lime zest, and lime juice in a small bowl. Season to taste with salt. Cover and refrigerate until ready to use or for up to 3 days.

Rinse fish and pat dry. Combine oil, vinegar, basil, oregano, garlic, salt, and pepper in a large heavy-duty plastic food bag. Add trout and seal bag securely. Rotate bag to distribute marinade and place in a shallow pan. Refrigerate for at least 1 hour or up to 2 hours, turning bag occasionally.

Meanwhile, to prepare Citrus Salsa, cut peel and white membrane from orange and grapefruit. Coarsely chop fruit and place in a large bowl. Stir in tomato, lime juice, orange juice, cilantro, and sugar. Season to taste with salt. Cover and refrigerate until ready to use.

Remove fish from bag and drain, discarding marinade. Arrange fish in center of cooking grate. Place lid on grill. Cook until fish is opaque but still moist in thickest part (10 to 12 minutes; cut to test). Using a wide metal spatula, transfer fish to a platter or individual plates. Serve with salsa and mayonnaise.

MAKES 4 SERVINGS.

Per serving: 579 calories (73% from fat), 47 g total fat (7 g saturated fat), 89 mg cholesterol, 367 mg sodium, 15 g carbohydrates, 2 g fiber, 25 g protein, 93 mg calcium, 2 mg iron

Yucatan Red Snapper

Here is a tomato sauce with authority, depth, and character. A whole red snapper cooked in the sauce is then sprinkled with olives and cilantro.

Charcoal	Indirect
Gas	Indirect/Medium Heat
Grilling time	40–50 minutes

2   tablespoons olive oil

1   large onion, chopped

2   cloves garlic, minced or pressed

4   teaspoons sugar

1   teaspoon salt

¼   teaspoon *each* ground cinnamon and ground cloves

5   cups (1.2 liters) peeled, seeded, and chopped tomatoes

1   tablespoon cornstarch mixed with 1½ teaspoons *each* lemon juice and water

1   or 2 fresh jalapeño chiles, seeded and minced

2   tablespoons drained canned capers

1   whole red snapper, rockfish, Pacific red snapper, or striped bass, 5 to 5½ pounds (2.3 to 2.5 kg), cleaned, scaled, and head removed

⅓   cup (80 ml) thinly sliced pimento-stuffed green olives

3   tablespoons minced cilantro

Lowfat

Heat oil in a wide frying pan over medium-high heat. Add onion and garlic and cook, stirring often, until onion begins to brown (about 10 minutes). Stir in sugar, salt, cinnamon, cloves, and tomatoes. Increase heat to high and cook, stirring, until mixture is thickened (5 to 8 minutes). Stir cornstarch mixture and add to pan. Cook, stirring, until mixture boils and liquid turns clear. Remove from heat and stir in chiles to taste and capers.

Rinse fish and pat dry. Place a piece of foil in a 9- by 13-inch (23- by 33-cm) metal pan. Lay fish lengthwise in pan (fish may overhang pan slightly) and pour sauce over fish. Set pan in center of cooking grate. Place lid on grill. Cook until fish is opaque but still moist in thickest part (40 to 50 minutes; cut to test).

Skim off watery juices from sauce; stir sauce to blend. Supporting fish with foil and a wide metal spatula, transfer fish to a platter. Sprinkle with olives and cilantro. Cut through fish to bone; lift off each serving with spatula. Spoon sauce from pan over individual servings.

MAKES 6 SERVINGS.

Per serving: 321 calories (25% from fat), 9 g total fat (1 g saturated fat), 76 mg cholesterol, 768 mg sodium, 15 g carbohydrates, 3 g fiber, 44 g protein, 93 mg calcium, 1 mg iron

GRILL BY THE BOOK
T I P

When fresh tomatoes are not at their peak of flavor, canned ones will work for salsas and sauces.

Scallops with Red Pepper Sauce

Grill scallops to juicy tenderness and serve them in a quick, simple, yet deliciously well-matched sauce.

Charcoal	Direct
Gas	Indirect/Medium Heat
Grilling time	5–8 minutes

¾ cup (180 ml) roasted red peppers, drained if necessary

½ cup (120 ml) chicken broth

¼ cup (60 ml) dry white wine

1 tablespoon minced fresh basil or ½ teaspoon dried basil

½ cup (120 ml) butter

1½ pounds (680 g) scallops, 1 to 1¾ inches (2.5 to 4.5 cm) in diameter

3 tablespoons butter, melted

Salt and pepper

In a blender or food processor, whirl peppers, broth, and wine until smooth. Pour into a wide frying pan. Add basil. Boil over high heat, stirring, until reduced to about ¾ cup/180 ml (about 5 minutes). Reduce heat to medium. Add the ½ cup (120 ml) butter in 1 chunk, stirring until incorporated. Remove sauce from heat and keep warm.

Rinse scallops and pat dry. Thread through their diameter on 4 skewers so they lie flat (larger scallops may require another skewer parallel to first). Brush generously with the melted butter.

Arrange skewers on cooking grate. Place lid on grill. Cook, turning once halfway through cooking time, until scallops are opaque but still moist in center (5 to 8 minutes; cut to test).

Pour sauce onto individual plates. Lay scallops in sauce. Season to taste with salt and pepper.

Makes 4 servings.

Per serving: 427 calories (66% from fat), 30 g total fat (18 g saturated fat), 134 mg cholesterol, 746 mg sodium, 6 g carbohydrates, 0 g fiber, 29 g protein, 55 mg calcium, 1 mg iron

Prawns with Prosciutto & Basil

Wrapped in prosciutto and basil, these superbly flavored prawns deserve a spotlight at your next party. Eat them as they come off the grill or refrigerate them for the following day.

Charcoal	Direct
Gas	Indirect/Medium Heat
Marinating time	15 minutes–4 hours
Grilling time	6–8 minutes

16   to 20 colossal prawns, 10 to 15 per pound (455 g), shelled (except for tails) and deveined

½   cup (120 ml) dry white wine

¼   cup (60 ml) balsamic vinegar

2   tablespoons extra-virgin olive oil

2   cloves garlic, minced or pressed

8   to 10 thin slices prosciutto, about 7 ounces (200 g) *total*

16   to 20 large basil leaves, rinsed and drained

Rinse prawns and pat dry. Combine wine, vinegar, oil, and garlic in a large heavy-duty plastic food bag or nonreactive bowl; remove and set aside 3 tablespoons of the marinade. Add prawns to bag and seal (or cover bowl). Rotate bag to distribute marinade and place in a shallow pan. Refrigerate for at least 15 minutes or up to 4 hours, turning prawns occasionally.

Cut prosciutto in half lengthwise. Remove prawns from bag and drain, discarding marinade in bag. Lay a basil leaf on each prawn; then wrap a prosciutto slice tightly around each, leaving tail exposed. Thread 4 or 5 prawns on each of 4 single- or double-pronged skewers.

Arrange skewers on cooking grate. Place lid on grill. Cook, turning once halfway through cooking time, until prawns are opaque in thickest part (6 to 8 minutes; cut to test). Transfer to a platter and drizzle with reserved marinade. Serve warm or cool. If made ahead, cover and refrigerate until next day.

MAKES 4 SERVINGS.

Per serving: 344 calories (45% from fat), 16 g total fat (3 g saturated fat), 241 mg cholesterol, 1116 mg sodium, 4 g carbohydrates, 0 g fiber, 41 g protein, 122 mg calcium, 5 mg iron

Skewered Shrimp with Lemon Pesto

Grated lemon zest gives a bright burst of flavor to the pesto marinade for these grilled shrimp. Serve them with freshly cooked vermicelli and a green salad or thread them individually onto bamboo skewers to make wonderful appetizers.

Charcoal	Direct
Gas	Indirect/Medium Heat
Marinating time	30 minutes–4 hours
Grilling time	4–5 minutes

Lemon Pesto (see below)

32   large shrimp, 1 to 1¼ pounds (455 to 565 g) *total,* shelled (except for tails) and deveined

Basil sprigs

Lemon Pesto

½   cup (120 ml) firmly packed fresh basil

¼   cup (60 ml) olive oil

2   tablespoons *each* grated lemon zest and grated Parmesan cheese

1   clove garlic

1   tablespoon pine nuts

In a food processor or blender, combine ingredients for Lemon Pesto. Whirl until smooth. Rinse shrimp and pat dry. Place in a large heavy-duty plastic food bag or nonreactive bowl. Pour in pesto and seal bag (or cover bowl). Rotate bag to distribute marinade and place in a shallow pan. Refrigerate for at least 30 minutes or up to 4 hours, turning shrimp occasionally.

Remove shrimp from bag and drain, discarding marinade. Thread shrimp on skewers. Arrange skewers on cooking grate. Place lid on grill. Cook, turning once halfway through cooking time, until shrimp are opaque in thickest part (4 to 5 minutes; cut to test). Transfer to a platter or individual plates. Garnish with basil sprigs.

MAKES 4 SERVINGS.

Per serving: 249 calories (62% from fat), 17 g total fat (3 g saturated fat), 142 mg cholesterol, 184 mg sodium, 3 g carbohydrates, 0 g fiber, 21 g protein, 136 mg calcium, 3 mg iron

Very Easy

GRILL BY THE BOOK
TIP

To prevent the lemon seeds from falling into food, wrap lemon halves in cheesecloth; then squeeze.

Easy Side Dishes for Fish & Shellfish

When you want a lowfat side dish to serve with naturally lean fish or shellfish, try one of the choices on these pages. Most are easy-to-prepare recipes that can be made quickly. Some can even be served together; consider pairing the corn salad with one of the grilled vegetable recipes.

Corn Salad with Three-Herb Dressing

½   cup (120 ml) white wine vinegar

¼   cup (60 ml) salad oil

4   teaspoons Dijon mustard

2   teaspoons sugar

4   cups (950 ml) corn kernels cut from steamed corn (6 or 7 ears)

½   cup (120 ml) *each* finely chopped fresh mint and cilantro

¼   cup (60 ml) finely chopped fresh dill

    Salt and pepper

1   large avocado

1   large tomato, cut into 12 wedges

    Mint, cilantro, or dill sprigs

In a large bowl, whisk vinegar, oil, mustard, and sugar until blended. Stir in corn and chopped mint, cilantro, and dill. Season to taste with salt and pepper. Mound corn salad on a platter. Pit and peel avocado; cut into 12 wedges. Arrange avocado and tomato wedges around salad. Garnish with mint sprigs.

Makes 6 servings.

Per serving: 222 calories (50% from fat), 13 g total fat (2 g saturated fat), 0 mg cholesterol, 104 mg sodium, 16 g carbohydrates, 4 g fiber, 4 g protein, 20 mg calcium, 1 mg iron

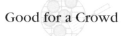

Good for a Crowd

Grilled Zucchini Ribbons with Thyme

Charcoal	Direct
Gas	Indirect/Medium Heat
Cooking time	7–8 minutes

1½   tablespoons minced fresh thyme

1   tablespoon olive oil

1½   teaspoons lemon juice

1   clove garlic, minced

4   medium-size zucchini

    Salt

In a small bowl, combine thyme, oil, lemon juice, and garlic; set aside.

With a sharp knife, slice zucchini lengthwise into ¼-inch (6-mm) strips. Sprinkle lightly with salt. Arrange zucchini on cooking grate. Place lid on grill. Cook, turning once halfway through cooking time, until zucchini is tender when pierced (7 or 8 minutes). With a wide metal spatula, transfer zucchini to a platter. Drizzle with thyme mixture.

Makes 4 to 6 servings.

Per serving: 66 calories (71% from fat), 6 g total fat (1 g saturated fat), 0 mg cholesterol, 4 mg sodium, 4 g carbohydrates, 1 g fiber, 1 g protein, 24 mg calcium, 1 mg iron

Very Easy

Marinated Vegetable Grill

Charcoal	Indirect
Gas	Indirect/Medium Heat
Marinating time	1–6 hours
Cooking time	40 minutes

3   onions, about 3 inches (8 cm) in diameter, unpeeled, cut in half crosswise

3   *each* large red and green bell peppers

3   or 4 medium-size tomatoes

½   cup (120 ml) red wine vinegar

¼   cup (60 ml) olive oil

2   cloves garlic, minced or pressed

2   tablespoons drained capers

¼   teaspoon pepper

Arrange onions, cut side down, on cooking grate. Place lid on grill. Cook for 10 minutes. Add bell peppers and tomatoes. Cook, turning bell peppers and tomatoes occasionally, until charred in spots and soft when pressed (about 30 more minutes). Let cool briefly. Meanwhile, combine vinegar, oil, garlic, capers, pepper, and ¼ cup (60 ml) water in a small bowl; set aside.

Peel, core, and seed bell peppers. Core tomatoes. Cut off ends and slip outer skin from onions. Arrange vegetables in a shallow dish and stir in caper mixture. Cover and let stand for at least 1 hour or up to 6 hours.

MAKES 6 SERVINGS.

Per serving: 182 calories (45% from fat), 10 g total fat (1 g saturated fat), 0 mg cholesterol, 87 mg sodium, 24 g carbohydrates, 5 g fiber, 3 g protein, 40 mg calcium, 1 mg iron

Thai Noodle Salad

Chile Dressing (see below)

8   ounces (230 g) dried capellini or thin rice noodles

1   medium-size cucumber, seeded and cut into thin slivers

1   medium-size red bell pepper, cut into thin slivers

⅓   cup (80 ml) *each* thinly sliced green onions, chopped cilantro, and chopped fresh basil

Chile Dressing

½   cup (120 ml) rice vinegar or wine vinegar

¼   cup (60 ml) soy sauce

1   tablespoon *each* sugar, minced fresh ginger, and Oriental sesame oil

½   to 1 teaspoon crushed red pepper flakes

1   clove garlic, minced or pressed

In a small bowl, combine ingredients for Chile Dressing; set aside.

In a 4- to 5-quart (4- to 5-liter) pan, bring 2 quarts (1.9 liters) water to a boil over high heat. Stir in pasta, reduce heat to medium-high, and cook just until tender to bite (about 4 minutes for capellini, 2 to 3 minutes for rice noodles). Drain, rinse with cold water until cool, and drain again. Pour into a wide, shallow bowl. Top with cucumber, bell pepper, onions, cilantro, and basil. Add dressing and lift with 2 forks to mix.

MAKES 4 SERVINGS.

Per serving: 292 calories (13% from fat), 5 g total fat (1 g saturated fat), 0 mg cholesterol, 1037 mg sodium, 54 g carbohydrates, 3 g fiber, 9 g protein, 64 mg calcium, 4 mg iron

Lowfat

Prawns with Corn & Black Bean Salad

Flavors, textures, and colors harmonize beautifully in this festive offering:
Toasted triangles of cornbread, wedges of avocado, and a black bean and grilled corn salad
accompany skewers of prawns, which have been marinated in a honey-citrus mixture.

Charcoal	Direct
Gas	Indirect/Medium Heat
Marinating time	30 minutes–6 hours
Grilling time	About 2–5 minutes

16 colossal prawns, 10 to 15 per pound (455 g), shelled and deveined

Honey-Lime Marinade (see below)

6 tablespoons olive oil

3 medium-size ears yellow or white corn, husks and silk removed

1 can, about 15 ounces (425 g), black beans, drained

½ cup (120 ml) thinly sliced green onions

1 tablespoon minced cilantro

1 baked cornbread, about 8 inches (20 cm) square

1 large avocado

Cilantro sprigs

Honey-Lime Marinade

1 teaspoon grated lime zest

⅓ cup (80 ml) lime juice

2 tablespoons distilled white vinegar

1 tablespoon honey

2 teaspoons Dijon mustard

1 teaspoon ground cumin

2 cloves garlic, minced or pressed

1 fresh jalapeño chile, seeded and minced

Rinse prawns and pat dry. In a small bowl, combine ingredients for Honey-Lime Marinade. Pour ⅓ cup (80 ml) of the marinade into a large heavy-duty plastic food bag or nonreactive bowl; set aside remaining marinade. Add prawns and seal bag (or cover bowl). Rotate bag to distribute marinade and place in a shallow pan. Refrigerate for at least 30 minutes or up to 6 hours, turning prawns occasionally. Meanwhile, combine reserved marinade with oil; cover and set aside.

Arrange corn on cooking grate. Place lid on grill. Cook, turning occasionally, until lightly browned (about 15 minutes). Meanwhile, remove prawns from bag and drain, discarding marinade in bag. Thread 4 prawns on each of 4 skewers; set aside.

Remove corn from grill and let cool. Cut corn off cob and place kernels in a large bowl. Stir in beans, onions, minced cilantro, and reserved marinade-oil mixture; set aside.

Cut cornbread into 4 squares; cut each piece diagonally and split horizontally. Arrange bread, cut side down, on cooking grate. Place lid on grill. Cook until toasted on bottom (about 1 minute). Turn bread and cook until other side is toasted (about 1 more minute). Remove and keep warm.

Arrange prawns on cooking grate. Place lid on grill. Cook, turning once halfway through cooking time, until prawns are opaque in thickest part (6 to 8 minutes; cut to test). Meanwhile, cut avocado in half, pit, and peel; cut each half in half again.

Mound corn salad on a platter or individual plates and add prawns and avocado. Garnish with cilantro sprigs. Serve with cornbread.

MAKES 4 SERVINGS.

Per serving: 850 calories (43% from fat), 41 g total fat (6 g saturated fat), 210 mg cholesterol, 1150 mg sodium, 85 g carbohydrates, 9 g fiber, 41 g protein, 289 mg calcium, 9 mg iron

GRILL BY THE BOOK
T I P

Brush cut avocado with lemon or lime juice to prevent discoloration.

Colossal Prawns

Big and dramatic, but with a price tag to match—are giant prawns worth their cost?
They are when you want a smashing presentation. These behemoths take well to a variety of
preparations. Here are three guest-worthy options.

Charcoal	Direct
Gas	Indirect/Medium Heat
Marinating time	30 minutes–2 hours
Grilling time	3–5 minutes

1 to 1¼ pounds (455 to 565 g) colossal prawns, 10 to 15 per pound (455 g), or extra-colossal prawns, 8 to 10 per pound (455 g), shelled and deveined

¼ cup (60 ml) dry sherry

¼ cup (60 ml) rice vinegar or cider vinegar

2 tablespoons Oriental sesame oil

1 tablespoon minced fresh ginger

2 teaspoons sugar

1 teaspoon soy sauce

1 teaspoon finely shredded orange zest

3 small oranges

3½ quarts (3.3 liters) bite-size pieces of spinach leaves, rinsed and crisped

1 large red bell pepper, cut into thin slivers

Salt and pepper

Prawns & Tomatoes with Basil Oil

Prawns & Spinach Salad

Cut down back of each prawn almost but not completely through. Rinse and pat dry.

In a small bowl, combine sherry, vinegar, oil, ginger, sugar, soy sauce, and orange zest. Place prawns in a large heavy-duty plastic food bag or nonreactive bowl. Add 2 tablespoons of the marinade and seal bag (or cover bowl); set aside remaining marinade. Rotate bag to distribute marinade and place in a shallow pan. Refrigerate for at least 30 minutes or up to 2 hours, turning prawns occasionally.

Cut peel and white membrane from oranges. Thinly slice fruit crosswise; cut slices in half. Place in a large serving bowl with spinach and bell pepper. Cover and refrigerate until cold or for up to 1 hour.

Remove prawns from bag and drain, discarding marinade. Spread prawns out flat on cooking grate. Place lid on grill. Cook, turning once halfway through cooking time, until prawns are opaque in thickest part (3 to 5 minutes; cut to test). Gently stir shrimp and reserved marinade into salad mixture. Season to taste with salt and pepper.

MAKES 4 SERVINGS.

Per serving: 271 calories (31% from fat), 9 g total fat (1 g saturated fat), 159 mg cholesterol, 299 mg sodium, 21 g carbohydrates, 5 g fiber, 24 g protein, 169 mg calcium, 5 mg iron

Charcoal	Direct
Gas	Indirect/Medium Heat
Grilling time	6–10 minutes

Bacon strips (1 for each prawn)

16 colossal prawns, 10 to 15 per pound (455 g), or 8 extra-colossal prawns, 8 to 10 per pound (455 g), shelled (except for tails) and deveined

Prawns Wrapped in Bacon

In a wide frying pan, cook bacon, a portion at a time, over medium-high heat, turning often, until some of the fat cooks out but bacon is still limp (about 3 minutes). Drain on paper towels.

Rinse prawns and pat dry. Wrap each with a piece of bacon. Arrange prawns in pairs on a flat surface, with head ends hooked around one another and tails pointing in opposite directions. On 2 parallel skewers, thread a pair of extra-colossal or 2 pairs of colossal prawns (prawns should lie flat). Repeat for remaining prawns.

Arrange skewers on cooking grate. Place lid on grill. Cook, turning once halfway through cooking time, until bacon is crisp and prawns are opaque in thickest part (6 to 10 minutes; cut prawns to test).

MAKES 4 SERVINGS.

Per serving: 270 calories (50% from fat), 14 g total fat (5 g saturated fat), 200 mg cholesterol, 578 mg sodium, 1 g carbohydrates, 0 g fiber, 32 g protein, 64 mg calcium, 3 mg iron

Charcoal	Direct
Gas	Indirect/Medium Heat
Grilling time	6–10 minutes

1 to 1¼ pounds (455 to 565 g) colossal prawns, 10 to 15 per pound (455 g), or extra-colossal prawns, 8 to 10 per pound (455 g), shelled and deveined

¼ cup (60 ml) extra-virgin olive oil

1 clove garlic, minced or pressed

2 tablespoons minced fresh basil or 1 teaspoon dried basil

3 large tomatoes, sliced crosswise about ½ inch (1 cm) thick

4 large romaine lettuce leaves, rinsed and crisped

Basil sprigs

Salt and pepper

Prawns & Tomatoes with Basil Oil

Rinse prawns and pat dry. Thread on 4 skewers. In a small bowl, combine oil, garlic, and minced basil. Brush prawns and tomato slices all over with basil oil.

Arrange prawns and tomatoes on cooking grate. Place lid on grill. Cook, turning once and brushing with basil oil halfway through cooking time, until tomatoes are hot and prawns are opaque in thickest part (6 to 10 minutes; cut prawns to test).

Place a romaine leaf on each of 4 plates. Arrange tomatoes and prawns on plates. Drizzle with any remaining basil oil. Garnish with basil sprigs. Season to taste with salt and pepper.

MAKES 4 SERVINGS.

Per serving: 267 calories (54% from fat), 16 g total fat (2 g saturated fat), 159 mg cholesterol, 170 mg sodium, 159 g carbohydrates, 2 g fiber, 23 g protein, 76 mg calcium, 4 mg iron

CLAMBAKE ON THE GRILL

Clambakes are traditional on the Atlantic coast. Deep pits are dug in the sand and lined with coals and wood; then tubs of seaweed-layered vegetables and shellfish are lowered in and steamed. For a nontraditional clambake in the garden, a barbecue can cook the food for you, but the food won't steam; instead, it smokes.

This clambake features clams, corn, potatoes, onions, lobsters, and sausages. For dipping, there's a lean vinegar sauce in place of melted butter.

Heat loaves of sliced French bread on another grill or in the oven. Wonderful summertime dessert ideas include angel food cake with fresh strawberries or ice cream sandwiched between homemade brownies.

Clambake on the Grill

Charcoal	Indirect
Gas	Indirect/Medium Heat
Grilling time	About 40 minutes

2	pounds (905 g) small clams, scrubbed
¼	cup (60 ml) cornmeal
	Mignonette Sauce (see below)
4	large ears corn, unhusked
2	cups (470 ml) hickory wood chips
16	small red-skinned potatoes, about 1½ inches (3.5 cm) in diameter
4	small lobsters, about 1¼ pounds (565 g) *each*
2	medium-size onions, unpeeled, cut in half
4	mild Italian sausages, about 1 pound (455 g) *total*

Mignonette Sauce

1	cup (240 ml) white wine vinegar
¼	cup (60 ml) finely diced red or yellow bell pepper
2	tablespoons minced shallots
1	clove garlic, minced or pressed
¼	teaspoon coarsely ground black pepper

Combine clams and cornmeal in a large bowl of water; set aside in a cool place for 2 hours. Drain and rinse clams. Meanwhile, combine ingredients for Mignonette Sauce in a small bowl; set aside.

Make sure corn husks enclose cobs completely and are tightly closed at top. Immerse corn in cold water to cover for about 30 minutes. Meanwhile, place wood chips in a bowl; add enough warm water to make them float; let soak for 30 minutes.

In a 2- to 3-quart (1.9- to 2.8-liter) pan, bring 1 quart (950 ml) water to a boil over high heat. Add potatoes; reduce heat, cover, and simmer until potatoes are tender but still somewhat crisp in center (about 15 minutes). Drain and set aside.

In a 10- to 12-quart (10- to 12-liter) pan, bring 6 quarts (6 liters) water to a rapid boil over high heat. Picking up 1 lobster at a time, hold body from top and plunge headfirst into water (cook 2 lobsters at a time). Return water to a boil; reduce heat, cover, and simmer for 5 minutes. Using tongs, lift lobsters from pan and let cool briefly. Twist 2 large claws free from body; drain claws and bodies and set aside.

In a charcoal barbecue, drain wood chips and scatter onto coals close to a side of barbecue. *In a gas barbecue,* place chips in a foil pan and set under cooking grate on top of heat source in left front corner of barbecue; turn heat to high and preheat for 10 to 15 minutes.

Place onions, cut side down, on sides of cooking grate but not over heat source. Place lid on grill. (*In a gas barbecue,* turn heat to Indirect/Medium.) Cook for 10 minutes. Arrange sausages and lobsters in center of cooking grate. Drain corn and place over lobsters. Lay potatoes around and over corn. Cook for 20 more minutes. Arrange clams directly over heat source. Cook until clam shells pop open (about 10 more minutes). Discard any clams that have not opened.

Serve with sauce for dipping.

MAKES 4 SERVINGS.

Per serving: 661 calories (32% from fat), 24 g total fat (8 g saturated fat), 166 mg cholesterol, 1288 mg sodium, 59 g carbohydrates, 7 g fiber, 54 g protein, 135 mg calcium, 8 mg iron

Good for a Crowd

Ginger-Chile Basted Crab

Removing the back shells of the crabs during grilling allows the wonderfully spicy, slightly sweet basting mixture to penetrate into the succulent meat.
If Dungeness crabs are unavailable, substitute a dozen jumbo blue crabs.

Charcoal	Direct
Gas	Indirect/Medium Heat
Grilling time	10–12 minutes

¼ cup (60 ml) seasoned rice wine vinegar, or ¼ cup (60 ml) white wine vinegar mixed with 2½ teaspoons sugar

2 tablespoons salad oil

1 tablespoon minced fresh ginger

1 large fresh jalapeño chile, seeded and minced

2 cloves garlic, minced or pressed

2 tablespoons minced cilantro

1 medium-size tomato, finely chopped

2 large live Dungeness crabs, about 2½ pounds (1.15 kg) *each*

In a small nonreactive bowl, combine vinegar, oil, ginger, chile, garlic, cilantro, and tomato; set aside.

In a 10- to 12-quart (10- to 12-liter) pan, bring 6 quarts (6 liters) water to a rapid boil over high heat. Picking up 1 crab at a time, hold crabs from rear and plunge headfirst into water. Return water to a boil; reduce heat, cover, and simmer for 5 minutes.

Using tongs, lift crabs from pan and let cool briefly. Pull off and discard triangular belly tab. Lift off shell from rear; rinse and set aside, if desired. Pull off and discard red membrane with entrails on body and soft gills. Rinse body well and drain.

Arrange crabs on cooking grate. Place lid on grill. Cook, brushing occasionally with ginger mixture and turning once halfway through cooking time, until meat in leg is opaque (10 to 12 minutes; crack open to test).

Transfer crabs to a platter. Spoon remaining ginger mixture over crabs; top with reserved back shells, if desired.

MAKES 4 SERVINGS.

Per serving: 201 calories (38% from fat), 8 g total fat (1 g saturated fat), 80 mg cholesterol, 976 mg sodium, 7 g carbohydrates, 0 g fiber, 24 g protein, 70 mg calcium, 1 mg iron

Lobster with Orange Aioli

Aioli is a garlicky mayonnaise-based sauce that graces many fish dishes in southern France. This citrus-scented version is an ideal partner for grilled lobster.

Charcoal	Direct
Gas	Indirect/Medium Heat
Grilling time	8–10 minutes

½	cup (120 ml) mayonnaise
2	cloves garlic, minced or pressed
1¾	teaspoons finely shredded orange zest
1½	tablespoons orange juice
1½	teaspoons lemon juice
1	tablespoon minced fresh tarragon or ¾ teaspoon dried tarragon
2	live American lobsters, about 2 pounds (905 g) *each*
¼	cup (60 ml) butter, melted
	Orange wedges
	Tarragon sprigs

In a small bowl, combine mayonnaise, garlic, ¾ teaspoon of the orange zest, orange juice, lemon juice, and minced tarragon. Cover and refrigerate aioli for at least 1 hour or up to 2 days.

In a 10- to 12-quart (10- to 12-liter) pan, bring 6 quarts (6 liters) water to a rapid boil over high heat. Picking up 1 lobster at a time, hold body from top and plunge headfirst into water. Return water to a boil; reduce heat, cover, and simmer for 5 minutes.

Using tongs, lift lobsters from pan and let cool briefly. Split lengthwise through back shell. Remove and discard stomach sac, intestinal vein, green tomalley (liver), and any coral-colored roe from each lobster. Rinse lobsters well and drain.

In a small bowl, combine butter and remaining orange zest. Brush lobsters all over with some of the butter mixture. Arrange lobsters on cooking grate. Place lid on grill. Cook, turning once and brushing with remaining butter mixture halfway through cooking time, until meat is opaque throughout (8 to 10 minutes; cut to test).

Transfer lobsters to a platter. Garnish with orange wedges and tarragon sprigs. Serve with aioli.

MAKES 4 SERVINGS.

Per serving: 404 calories (76% from fat), 34 g total fat (10 g saturated fat), 119 g cholesterol, 654 mg sodium, 4 g carbohydrates, 0 g fiber, 21 g protein, 78 mg calcium, 1 mg iron

How to Eat a Lobster

Provide plenty of napkins and set out finger bowls with a lemon slice in each. Also put out one or two large bowls for discarding shells.

Holding the lobster over the bowl, turn it soft side up and twist off the tail. Slide a fork between the soft underside of the tail and the meat and firmly pull out the meat. Crack open the claws using a heavy cracker. Pluck out the meat with a small lobster fork or a metal pick.

Twist the 8 small legs from the body and lift off the top body shell. Edible portions are the small quantity of meat, the greenish tomalley (liver), and any coral-colored roe. Suck the meat from the legs.

GRILL BY THE BOOK
TIP

To maximize flavor from citrus peels, use only the zest, or colored part; it holds the fragrant oils of the fruit.

Sage-buttered Lobster Tails

Barely a drop of this delicious sage butter is wasted, because the lobster tails are split lengthwise and grilled and served in their shells. Grilled crookneck squash is also brushed with the butter and accompanies the lobster to the table.

Charcoal	Direct
Gas	Indirect/Medium Heat
Grilling time	About 8 minutes

4   uncooked spiny lobster tails, 8 to 10 ounces (230 to 285 g) *each,* thawed if frozen

4   medium-size crookneck squash

¼   cup (60 ml) butter, melted

1   teaspoon grated lemon zest

2   tablespoons lemon juice

2   tablespoons minced fresh sage or 1 teaspoon dried sage

     Sage sprigs (optional)

     Lemon wedges

     Salt and pepper

With kitchen scissors, cut off fins and sharp spines on lobster tails. Set tails, shell side down, on a board; with a heavy knife, split in half lengthwise, using a hammer or mallet to force knife through shells. Rinse lobsters and pat dry.

Starting about ½ inch (1 cm) from stem end, cut each squash lengthwise 3 or 4 times, leaving pieces attached at stem end. Gently fan slices out.

In a small bowl, combine butter, lemon zest, lemon juice, and minced sage. Brush lobster and squash with half the butter mixture. Arrange lobster, shell side down, and squash, gently fanning out slices, on cooking grate. Place lid on grill. Cook, turning food once and brushing with more of the butter mixture halfway through cooking time, until squash is tender when pierced and lobster is opaque in thickest part (about 8 minutes; cut lobster to test).

Transfer lobster and squash to individual plates. Drizzle with remaining butter mixture and garnish with sage sprigs, if desired, and lemon wedges. Season to taste with salt and pepper.

MAKES 4 SERVINGS.

Per serving: 259 calories (44% from fat), 13 g total fat (7 g saturated fat), 132 mg cholesterol, 653 mg sodium, 6 g carbohydrates, 0 g fiber, 30 g protein, 117 mg calcium, 1 mg iron

Oysters with Tomatillo Salsa

*You won't need to struggle to open these oysters—they'll pop
open by themselves on the grill. The recipe works either as an appetizer or a main course.
Look for canned tomatillos in a Mexican market or in a well-stocked grocery store.*

Charcoal	Direct
Gas	Indirect/Medium Heat
Grilling time	About 8 minutes

Tomatillo Salsa (see below)

48   small oysters, 2 to 3 inches (5 to 8 cm) wide

Tomatillo Salsa

2   cans, about 13 ounces (370 g) *each,* tomatillos, drained and chopped

1   can, about 4 ounces (115 g), diced green chiles

½   cup (120 ml) *each* minced green onions and minced cilantro

2   tablespoons lime juice

Salt

Good for a Crowd

To prepare Tomatillo Salsa, combine tomatillos, chiles, onions, cilantro, and lime juice in a large bowl. Season to taste with salt. Cover and refrigerate until ready to use or for up to 2 days.

Scrub oysters with a stiff brush under cool running water. Arrange oysters, cupped side down, on cooking grate. Place lid on grill. Cook until shells pop open (about 8 minutes); remove oysters when shells open, protecting your hands with tongs or hot pads. Discard any oysters that have not opened.

Cut oysters free from shells, discarding top shells. Spoon tomatillo mixture over oysters and eat from shells.

MAKES 16 APPETIZER OR 6 MAIN-COURSE SERVINGS.

Per serving: 40 calories (18% from fat), 1 g total fat (0 g saturated fat), 17 mg cholesterol, 133 mg sodium, 5 g carbohydrates, 1 g fiber, 2 g protein, 17 mg calcium, 3 mg iron

Index